EXPLORERS

HUAWEI STORIES

TIAN TAO
YIN ZHIFENG

Published by
LID Publishing Limited
The Record Hall, Studio 204,
16-16a Baldwins Gardens,
London EC1N 7RJ, UK

524 Broadway, 11th Floor, Suite 08-120
New York, NY 10012, US

info@lidpublishing.com
www.lidpublishing.com

A member of:

BPR
Business Publishers Roundtable

www.businesspublishersroundtable.com

Printed by CPI Group (UK) Ltd, Croydon CR0 4YY
ISBN: 978-1-911498-55-1

Cover and page design: Caroline Li & Matthew Renaudin

EXPLORERS

HUAWEI STORIES

TIAN TAO
YIN ZHIFENG

LONDON   MONTERREY
MADRID   SHANGHAI
MEXICO CITY   BOGOTA
NEW YORK   BUENOS AIRES
BARCELONA   SAN FRANCISCO

Contents

Opportunism is the Enemy of Innovation

By Tian Tao

Huawei's sense of
direction, management
philosophy, and
innovation strategy
are all built on the
fundamental assumption
that the world needs
networks, and that
demand for massive
data transmission
is growing.

Explorers is an account of 30 years of innovation within Huawei's research and development (R&D) team. Innovation and transformation are two of Huawei's most sharply honed competitive edges, paving the way for its ongoing growth and strength.

In the early 1990s, Huawei's founder Ren Zhengfei was keenly aware that, as China's economic development began to pick up speed, large-scale build-out of information and communication technology infrastructure was soon to follow. After all, bridging the digital divide is one of the primary means through which developing countries can escape the grip of poverty. A clear path had unfurled before Huawei, broad and brimming with creative potential. Driven by a commitment to this path, the company grew from a dozen employees to several thousand, and then to the 180,000 you see today.

For the past 30 years, Huawei has concentrated its resources on the R&D of its communications infrastructure, which the company calls the 'pipe'. It includes fixed-line and mobile telecommunications, optical transmission, and data communications. Huawei maintained this strategic focus even after the IT bubble burst in 2001.

Huawei's sense of direction, management philosophy, and innovation strategy are all built on the fundamental assumption that the world needs networks, and that demand for massive data transmission is growing. This assumption has proven to be correct, as has the strategy that evolved from it. And it's on this assumption that the company bet the farm, so to speak, which is undoubtedly a key factor behind its rise and the success it's enjoyed thus far. Thirty years ago, the rate of mobile device penetration was less than 1%. Today, it is greater than 100%.

Over the next 20 to 30 years, we will enter an era that revolves around video and cloud technology. This has been Huawei's acting hypothesis for the past five years, and is one that shows every sign of being correct. AT&T's acquisition of Time Warner is the perfect example: a reflection of the US's strategic ambitions in the global market and its broader plans for the future.

Ren Zhengfei's response to this acquisition was that "Huawei is still small potatoes" compared to other players in the US market. However, the massive digital deluge set in motion by US companies – including the boom of artificial intelligence and the internet of things – will require information pipes with extremely large capacity. This is a blue ocean for Huawei. To make the most of this opportunity, Huawei needs to fully leverage its leadership position and strengths, double down on data transmission, and develop customer and innovation strategies that are aligned with future trends.

Innovation relies on forward-looking theory, for innovation without theory is like a river without a source. It also needs to be driven by a correct set of values. Over the past 30 years, Huawei's innovation in technology and products has followed the same enduring law: customer centricity.

It's been this way throughout the company's history. In the voice era, Huawei was merely an imitator, following in the footsteps of other companies. In the digital era, Huawei grew to become a leader in innovation, from digital switches, optical transmission, and IP routers, to distributed base stations, SingleRAN base stations, and IP microwaves. Throughout this process, Huawei made very few miscalculations in innovation and strategy. The reason is simplicity itself: a singular and unadorned focus on customer needs, both the obvious and those waiting to be discovered.

Disruption is a given, and our only mainstay is innovation. To remain outside the realms of failure, every business organization should follow a simple, golden rule: put customers first, embrace disruption, and embrace innovation.

The recipient of the 2016 Nobel Prize for Literature, American singer Bob Dylan, once sang, "How many times must a man look up before he can see the sky?" I was reviewing the draft of this book when I heard these lyrics, and I couldn't help but feel a strong sense of resonance. He had described Huawei's path perfectly.

Twenty years ago, in a shabby rental apartment that doubled as Huawei's Shanghai Research Center, Ren Zhengfei was talking with a dozen or so young R&D engineers. He said that Huawei was going to build an R&D building that would accommodate 10,000 people within 20 years' time. Sure enough, less than 20 years later, Huawei's Shanghai Research Center is now housed in one of Asia's largest single-structure buildings and has more than 10,000 technical experts, engineers, and developers. It is also home to Huawei's leading wireless products.

Today, Huawei has 15 research centres, 28 centres of expertise, and 180,000 employees around the world. Almost half of Huawei's employees are involved in R&D. Every year, the company invests more than 10% of its revenue in R&D, having spent over ¥313 billion in the past decade.

Huawei believes that perseverance leads to strategic breakthroughs. Over the past 30 years, Huawei has gathered together one of the world's largest R&D teams, which maintains a laser-like focus on information pipes, throwing everything they have at innovation in this field. Wave after wave of ceaseless effort has helped them reach the top. The stories in this book are the stories of that effort – the persistence, bravery and undaunted spirit of Huawei's R&D team. They speak of clashes and mutual inspiration between some of the world's brightest minds as they charged out far beyond the beaten track.

Opportunism is the enemy of innovation. Huawei has rejected the wiles of easy money and the urge to spread itself too thin. Even in its own strategic domain, Huawei remains wary of diverting its limited strength and resources to the wrong areas, and has stayed on guard against the temptation of short-term interests. The Personal Handy-phone System (PHS) is a case in point. This technology, which had long been obsolete in Japan, had found its way into the Chinese market, where it became all the rage in the late 1990s. Had Huawei decided to take this opportunity, with just a small investment of a few dozen people and around ¥20 million, PHS could have brought in tens of billions of Chinese yuan in annual revenue. However, Ren Zhengfei rejected the opportunity outright.

Instead, he decided to place his bet on WCDMA – an air interface standard that would form the basis of 3G telecommunications networks. He faced tremendous pressure, from both internal and external sources. One day in 2002, when I was having tea with Mr Ren, he repeated the same sentiment over and over again: "Huawei is a company with ideals."

According to Liu Chuanzhi, the founder of Lenovo, Huawei "climbed Mount Everest from the north side" – its coldest and steepest slope. Under the banner of the company's ideals, driven forward by its core values, the Huawei team has been cast as an unstoppable force. And through 30 years of struggle, the company has finally reached the top of the first mountain in a long and daunting range.

As Benjamin Franklin said, "He that can have patience can have what he will."

Success is the winner's curse. Will Huawei feel the pull of vertigo as it stands atop Mount Everest? Will it step into that inevitable trap like so many of its forebears, who went from infancy to maturity, and then quickly fell into sharp decline?

Without a doubt, the company faces a number of challenges, and it's in need of drastic change. Around 2009, Huawei started showing symptoms of the diseases that plague large corporations, so it began implementing a series of experimental transformations in management philosophy, incentive structures, and organization to ward off the onset of further blight.

Only Huawei itself can spell the end of Huawei, not any of its competitors. An excessively stable organization will inevitably experience a loss of vitality. Huawei needs to stay vigilant in thought and action.

In October 2016, Huawei sent out a thunderous rallying cry: 2,000 senior R&D experts and managers who had worked at Huawei for 15 to 20 years were to be assigned to overseas markets. This was a major move for the organization. Li Ruihua, a professor at Taiwan's National Chengchi University, who has closely followed and studied Huawei for many years, remarked that, "Few large companies around the world would dare to do this, or could even manage it."

The greatest challenge of managing an organization is building the organization's ability to fight its natural tendencies. In other words, a company needs to take a series of measures that keep it well outside of its comfort zone to prevent entropy[1]. Over the past 30 years, Huawei has built up its organization around the second law of thermodynamics[2], developing the company into a dissipative structure[3] that can reduce entropy by exchanging energy with the outside world. If Huawei hopes to continue basking in the glory of success, it should stick with this philosophy.

In fact, this was the logic behind sending the 2,000 senior R&D experts and managers to the frontlines. There they could engage with customers face-to-face, gain an intimate understanding of their practical requirements, and unearth any as-yet-unrealized needs together. More importantly, these experts and managers could serve as a boost to the sales

1 Entropy is a measure of disorder. An increase in entropy is the natural tendency of all things in nature, which gradually shift from order to disorder, and ultimately dissolution and death. Huawei's founder likens the rapid decay of a company to a natural increase in entropy.

2 The second law of thermodynamics states that the total entropy of an isolated system can only increase over time.

3 The concept of dissipative structures was first proposed by Ilya Prigogine. When a system reaches maximum entropy, it is said to be in a state of thermodynamic equilibrium – a suspended, motionless state of heat death. Dissipative structures are open systems that are not in equilibrium. By exchanging matter and energy with the outside environment, the flow of entropy in a dissipative structure can go negative, which makes the system more ordered. In an attempt to build Huawei into a dissipative (and therefore a more ordered, enduring) structure, Huawei regularly employs large organizational transformations and forward-looking incentive structures to offset the organization's natural increase in entropy.

team, like giving a tiger wings, and help bring new life to the R&D team. Shaking things up helps keep the organization full of life and passion. Only by cultivating an internal cycle of revitalization can the company more effectively embrace disruption and chaos.

Over the past several years, many new concepts have emerged in Huawei's management lexicon. These include 'absorbing the energy of the universe over a cup of coffee', 'forging ahead into uncharted territory along multiple paths in multiple waves', 'blowing open the top of the company's talent pyramid', de Laval nozzles[4], the 'Contribute and Share' system, and 'blurring the boundaries between internal and external talent to build an ecosystem of shared benefits'. Behind all of these concepts, and the series of transformation programmes that derive from them, is Huawei's acute sensitivity to the threat of becoming a large and ailing corporation, and its attempt to find a cure: the active exploration of change and the unknown.

Black swans, chaos, turmoil, discontinuity, uncertainty ... all of these words are used to describe people's anxiety about the present and the future. Huawei's next 30 years are unfolding against this very backdrop. Rejecting change is a dead end. Huawei has no choice but to innovate. Change will inject vitality into the organization, and innovation will equip it to deal with uncertainty. Innovation will start and end with satisfying customers' overt needs and creatively uncovering their less-discernible needs. Throughout this process, the rules of the game will remain the same: Huawei must continue to focus on its core business and never waste strategic effort on non-strategic opportunities.

This is the story of Huawei's innovation in the voice and data eras. In the past, Huawei was a first-class follower. But as it steps forward into the video era, can Huawei become a global leader? Will it grow adept at predicting where the wind will blow, forecasting the evolution of the industry just as its founder hopes?

Let's sit back and see what happens.

4 de Laval nozzles are tubes that are pinched in the middle. They are often used in rocket engines to pressurize gas, which causes the gas to heat up, and then accelerate when released. In Huawei's management philosophy, the concept of a de Laval nozzle is used to describe the company's approach to making breakthroughs. Huawei focuses its R&D on very specific and finite areas in its core business, brings in outside talent as needed, and concentrates their efforts via core competency centres to drive fundamental breakthroughs.

From Lone Heroes to Heroic Teams

By Ryan Ding

Huawei started with switches before expanding into transmission networks, wireless networks, data communications, and then building a presence in IT and devices. Having become an industry leader across almost all communications products, people often ask me: How did Huawei manage this? I believe there are three major reasons: systems and processes, people, and culture.

From Reliance on Lone Heroes to Replicable Success

In its early days, Huawei's product development was no different from any other company. We didn't have a well-defined approach to product engineering, or advanced systems and processes. The success or failure of a project mainly depended on the smartness of its manager and on luck. We were entirely reliant on 'heroic' individuals. In other words, product development was full of uncertainty and chance.

In 1997, after visiting IBM and other leading companies, our CEO, Ren Zhengfei, decided to develop and improve our management systems. We introduced the Integrated Product Development (IPD) process so that we could systematically and consistently launch successful, competitive products that met our customers' needs. Mr Ren set the direction for that corporate transformation: copy the process first, and then codify and improve it. Copying was to better understand the process; codifying turned it a habit; and improving was to make it even better. It was painful at first, forcing our feet into American shoes, but, thanks to this process, we were able to change our product development from an artisan workshop into something large scale, process-based, manageable, and replicable.

In the early days, it seemed every Huawei employee had limitless energy and worked extremely hard, but they often shot off in different directions, like particles in Brownian motion. We needed to channel them so that their energies were flowing in the same direction. That's what IPD did. It changed erratic, random motion into an orderly flow.

IPD is a process that seeks to scientifically manage product development. It divides the whole process – from the time when a customer communicates their need to the time when the need is met – into a series of stages and decision checkpoints. And it defines the processes, standards, tools, and methodologies for each stage. Following the IPD process, developers can no longer do whatever they like beyong processes . All development activities are planned and managed. Everyone follows the processes and standards so that product development becomes controllable and transparent.

IPD starts with commercial viability. It emphasizes product portfolio management, focus, necessary trade-offs, end-to-end management, and teamwork. Development capabilities are built into the structure of the company to ensure that successful practices can be copied and used for other products. With IPD, success is no longer a matter of luck.

People Are Always the Most Valuable Asset

How important are people to a company? Let me first tell you a story. In 2006, we acquired a small company that developed a certain kind of processor. We bought the company's source code and all its documentation, but we didn't hire any of the development team. We thought that with the code and the documentation, we could develop products on our own. After two years, however, we had developed nothing. In 2008, we brought the company's core team members on board and very soon they had produced a product. This made us realize that people are the most valuable asset in a company. They are worth much more than source code, designs, and documentation.

We also realized that we should properly reward those valuable people. Competition in the future will be our talent against your talent. A company's ability to compete will depend on whether it is able to attract the best people. If we don't offer good opportunities or competitive compensation, we will not attract them.

Huawei is well aware of this, so we are willing to give people who create more value and make more contributions very competitive compensation and rewards.

Which is more important, people or machines? Some companies claim that people are very important, but they actually think their machines are more valuable. So, if their computers are slow, or the lab is short of equipment, they arrange for their staff to work in shifts. Huawei knows that people are more valuable than machines, and tools should serve people, not the other way around, so we 'arm our people to the teeth' with the best possible tools. And when our employees travel for business, we encourage them to go by plane and taxi. We want them to save on travel time and use their time creating value for the company.

Experts May Be Senior to Managers

Technical staff often have a question in the back of their minds: Should I become a manager, or should I stay on the technical side? In many companies, managers get promoted faster and receive higher compensation packages.

At Huawei, the most senior staff member in a department is not necessarily the manager. It could easily be an expert. For example, the director of one overseas research centre is at grade 22, but six or seven fellows (the most senior technical experts at Huawei) in that centre are between grades 22 and 24. Directors of research centres are not allowed to fly business class, but Fellows are. And these Fellows may receive higher salaries than their own director. We do this to make sure that Huawei remains equally strong on both the managerial and technical sides.

We offer Fellows competitive compensation, but salary is a private thing. Nobody else sees their paychecks. So, we thought about how to give Fellows more visible incentives. We found one practice worth emulating from the University of California, Berkeley. They have a policy: if a professor wins a Nobel Prize, they are given a special parking spot near their office with a sign saying 'NL', which stands for 'Nobel Laureate'. When we selected the first group of Fellows four years ago, we set out the policy: Fellows can fly business class.

However, we found that most of them didn't do so. They said they were embarrassed to fly business class when their managers and colleagues were not allowed to. So we issued an order requiring Fellows to use their business class seats, otherwise they would be 'penalized'. Of course, we didn't really intend to fine them. We wanted the Fellows to feel able to make use of this perk and realize that if they didn't fly business class, no one on the technical side of the company would feel the sense of prestige that their expertise deserves.

Build Where the People Are

One Huawei policy is that we should build centres of expertise (COEs) in places where there are talented people. Our facilities should go where the talent is, not the other way around. Some companies go out and bring people back to their home country. Huawei finds the best people worldwide and then sets up teams around them. We don't necessarily require them to work in China.

Our microwave COE is a case in point. We found a top leader in this field in Milan and decided to build a team there especially for him. We later established a research centre in Milan, which is now Huawei's global COE for microwave transmission.

Different environments make for different results. We believe that environment is a crucial factor in nurturing talented people and a person's creativity largely depends on their environment. In China, we have a saying, "Build a nest to attract phoenixes." But at Huawei, we believe that if you take a phoenix out of the environment that supports it, then what you end up with is not a phoenix, but a turkey.

Milan is the home of microwave. It has abundant talent, a mature industry, and many universities specialize in this field. In this environment, you can pick up plenty of information just by grabbing a coffee with your peers. What would happen if we brought the COE from Milan to China? China doesn't have a mature microwave industry, so our people wouldn't even know who to have coffee with.

Only Culture Endures

One important reason why Huawei has succeeded in product development is our core values and culture.

After I completed my graduate studies, I worked in another company before I joined Huawei. There was quite a contrast between the two. I found that at Huawei, all we have to do is focus on the customers and dedicate ourselves to our work. If we do that, our compensation and careers take care of themselves. We also don't have to worry about picking a clique or being on anyone's 'side': in our culture, everyone works towards the same goals.

Renato Lombardi, the head of Huawei's Milan Research Center, is Italian. He told me that Huawei's culture is the reason why many things that seem impossible in other companies become possible at Huawei. Huawei engineers may lack experience and make mistakes, but they are full of passion and work very hard. After a target is set, they will do everything they can to hit that target, no matter how difficult and challenging it is. They fail and try again, fail and try again, until they finally succeed. This is the Huawei culture.

Managers Are Promoted from Successful Teams

Huawei insists on choosing people from successful teams to promote to managerial positions. The more successful a team is, the more people from the team are likely to be promoted. For example, I used to manage the softswitch R&D team. After we achieved success with that product, my team members and I all got promoted. This way, the DNA of success gets spread through the company.

Mr Ren always emphasizes that we only select managers from successful teams, not failed teams. There are two reasons: first, everyone wants to learn from role models, so their influence is important; and, second, these outstanding managers pass on the best parts of our corporate culture.

Huawei Wants Engineers with Business Acumen

Huawei emphasizes that we need engineers with business insight. This means that our innovation is driven by customer needs, not just by technology. All our products must be commercially viable.

Huawei pursues excellence. When we decide to develop a product, we set very ambitious goals from the start and build future-proof competitive strengths at the highest level. For example, when we designed the Single Antenna Solution, we completely rejected the idea of a 'good enough' solution. We wanted to develop the best solution in the industry. Within just five years, Huawei's antenna solution became the industry leader.

Tolerating Failure and Mistakes

Not all Huawei products have succeeded. In 2002, our iNet was a complete failure. Five suppliers won contracts from the customer, but Huawei got nothing. Why? Because Huawei was too oriented towards technology and ignored what the customer said. The company didn't blame the individuals involved in that failure. They absorbed the shock and learned a valuable lesson. They realized that they must always focus on customer needs, and they shifted their orientation. In the end, Huawei's core network solution became the biggest seller in the world. This is a culture where failure is tolerated.

Some companies tell their R&D staff that the success or failure of their research projects will affect their entire careers. This kind of practice makes innovation impossible. Research is a trial-and-error process. There will be no innovation if no error

When we develop products, we are not aiming for short-term results. We have to look at long-term value. We need to invest in projects that may not bring immediate results.

is allowed. Who would dare to innovate if a mistake is going to haunt them for the rest of their life? Of course, we analyse the root causes after mistakes are made, but not so that we can find someone to hold accountable. We do it to learn the lesson and avoid repeating the same mistakes in the future.

Strategic Patience, No Opportunism

When we develop products, we are not aiming for short-term results. We have to look at long-term value. We need to invest in projects that may not bring immediate results. In 2008, for example, I decided to develop a chip. I told my team that we may not see the chip launched within my term in charge of that team. But I still decided to make the investment so that the company can remain competitive over the long term. I had transferred to the sales team, and then transferred back to R&D before the chip finally came out at the end of 2011.

What mechanisms push Huawei's product teams to make long-term investments? When we appraise a product line manager, we not only look at the product line's present performance; we also check whether the product line will be able to sustain its growth and competitive position two years after the manager leaves. If not, it means that the manager has sapped the product line's capacity.

Anyone Who Can Haul Himself Up Out of the Mud Is a Sage

Huawei emphasizes reflection on our own mistakes. In 2000, the R&D department held a huge conference, attended by about 10,000 employees, to reflect on the problem of obsolete inventory. Everyone there thought about the mistakes that they each had made and everyone received a special 'award' – the obsolete equipment and used tickets from unnecessary plane travel that had resulted from their own errors and inexperience.

Self-reflection helps product lines stay serious, stay humble, and keep learning from best industry practice. In 2010, we received a complaint from Telekom Malaysia about an accident caused by one of our products. The company organized reflection sessions at all levels of the organization. Everyone analysed the root causes and thought about how to make systematic improvements. These sessions helped us improve solution management and reinforced our customer-centric culture.

Reflection on the problem of obsolete inventory by Huawei's R&D team in 2000

One of the ways in which we stay self-reflective and critical is by setting up Blue Teams. Blue Teams are the simulated opposition to our winning Red Teams. Blue Teams research how to beat Huawei, our products and solutions. In other words, Blue Teams are there precisely to deflate us and to say the unpleasant truths. They are not there to make friends. One of our access network products illustrates how a Blue Team works at Huawei. The Red Team had designed a platform architecture for a European customer. An expert from the Blue Team wrote a long article saying that the architecture had many problems and would definitely fail. The expert also listed many reasons, with evidence and examples. The Red Team fought back. They brought in all the hardware and software experts they could find, and kept on refining the architecture and design to prove that their original concept was right. Thanks to the Blue Team's challenge, the Red Team worked much harder on the architecture. They started the design in 2004 and launched it in 2006. Today, ten years later, it is still one of the industry's leading architectures. The Blue Team mechanism helps to unleash our potential and inspire our people to keep innovating on our products and technologies.

We know that in today's world, no one can work alone. A product's success depends on a team. It needs a heroic team, not a lone hero. And to produce those heroic teams, we need effective management systems and processes, talented people, and the right culture. That is the only way to cultivate cohorts of heroes and reliably replicate our successes.

Pulling Ourselves Out of the Mud

By Yao Yiyu

"Huawei has no idea what a next-generation telecommunications network is like!" Our customer's criticism was like a punch in the gut.

In 2001, we managed to develop and launch our next-generation switch, iNET, in a stunningly short time. What awaited us was not ovation or praise, but harsh reality: the customer did not want our product in their network.

We had been totally rejected by our customer. The failure nearly destroyed Huawei's core network business. The great success of the C&C08 switch was wiped out. We had to start from square one, but what resources did we have to start with? How could we ever catch up?

Stuck in the Mud

The failure had to do with a choice we made. In 2000, with the rise of the internet and internet protocol (IP), there was disagreement over how telecommunications networks should evolve: ATM or IP. ATM stands for 'asynchronous transfer mode', which is a real-time, highly reliable transmission technology based on the telecom standards of the United Nations' International Telecommunication Union. IP is a simple internet-based transmission technology.

We had achieved great success with the C&C08 switch, so we believed that what customers needed was an ATM-based switch. IP-based softswitches were just for the IT sector, we thought. We didn't listen to our customers – in fact, when they told us about plans to move to softswitches, we argued with them. We even criticized our customers to their faces. As a result, our customers were very disappointed with our solution.

We had forgotten our customers' needs and been blinded by our overconfidence. Our product flopped and our huge investment was wasted, not to mention the work of hundreds of people over nearly two years. The core network product line was in jeopardy, and our R&D team was on the brink of being disbanded.

Back then, I was just a novice. I had only been with the company for five months. I never imagined that the first product I developed at Huawei would so quickly come to the end of its life. I was very upset and the future looked bleak. I didn't even know whether there was still going to be a job for me at Huawei.

Just as I was at my most desperate, I heard a piece of exciting news: the company was not giving up on us, but had decided to adjust its strategy. We were going to shift immediately to IP technology and rebuild our platform. We may have been stuck in the mud, but at least we had a glimmer of hope.

Now the pressure was really on. The only way to rescue our reputation was to succeed in our new mission.

For the new platform, we selected a new, all-IP hardware architecture. Starting from scratch, we had to finish building the operating system, database, communications functions, and all other basic functions within less than a year. In our planning meeting, the product manager kept asking us: "Can you deliver it on schedule?"

Our platform project manager, Li Huabin, said, "We guarantee we will not delay this product."

I was in charge of the operating system. It was the first time that I had worked on the operating system. I quaked when I saw the huge, thick manuals I had to study, all in English. When I went home for the Spring Festival, I spent the whole time reading the manuals. My parents started to worry and wondered if I was recovering from a broken heart or some other emotional distress. Under heavy pressure, I learned rapidly. Just one and a half months later, I was the team's expert on fixing crashed systems.

Li Huabin took the most complex, most challenging part of the project: developing the IP communications module. He also led the commissioning of the platform and products. He was our team firefighter, too: putting out fires wherever they flared up. When we finally succeeded and placed the first call through the new system, the strain finally got the better of him, and he immediately fell ill. When people asked him why he had worked

After we returned to
our path of putting
customers first, our
customers chose
to give us another
chance, and we finally
won their recognition
and regained our
position in the
Chinese market.

so hard, he said he didn't want to see the platform fail while it was in his charge.

In 2003, our softswitch platform gradually took shape, as we added more and more basic architectures and technologies. It had high-capacity, distributed architecture able to support millions of users. Reliability was at the five-nines level (99.999% reliability) that carrier networks require. And the switching technology was all-IP. These star features meant that our products far outshone our competitors' in terms of both the technology used and the performance achieved.

After we returned to our path of putting customers first, our customers chose to give us another chance, and we finally won their recognition and regained our position in the Chinese market. We had paid a hefty price for ignoring their needs. This important lesson made us realize that to build a competitive solution, we must focus on our customers first. Our products can only succeed when they truly solve customer problems.

Satellites Under Attack

When that first-generation platform was put into operation, I became the maintenance manager of the platform. But, at the time, we lacked the ability to diagnose problems and provide remote support, which caused a few embarrassing situations. In 2005, a telecom operator in Madagascar complained that when calls were routed through our equipment, voice quality on their networks often deteriorated, and sometimes there was no sound at all. The operator was using satellites for relay transmission for their high-value tourist users, and they were very worried: with such poor signal quality, what if they lost their customers? They asked us to figure out a solution as soon as possible.

We performed simulation tests over and over again, but failed to reproduce the problem. At first, we thought it was because of weak satellite signals, or disconnection of the satellite links due to interference by the weather or geomagnetic storms.

However, our message tracing told us that this was not the cause. According to the message trace, the messages were successfully sent out, but somehow went missing while being transmitted over the satellite links, and the other end of the link didn't receive any signal.

Why was this happening? Was it because the satellites had been hit by space debris? We didn't rule out anything, no matter how unlikely it might seem. We bit the bullet and asked the customer: "Could you please check whether there is any problem with the satellites?"

The customer was very confused. "If the satellites have been attacked," they replied, "why is it only the phone signals that are being affected? The message trace is not telling us anything. Can you use a third-party tool to find a more convincing explanation for these failures?"

We had to send out our signalling expert, Huang Long, to capture packets with a signal analyser. Huang was a brilliant engineer, but this was his first time leaving China. He had a very thick accent and didn't dress like a highly skilled professional and, as a result, he was stopped at the border. When the plane took off, he hadn't even managed to get his boarding card. After much effort, the company was finally able to get him another ticket. He arrived in Madagascar two days later. We were waiting with our hearts in our mouths. The whole process made us even more determined to develop the ability to run message tracing remotely.

We finally found the root cause. It was that message transmission took too long over the satellite link. Sometimes it exceeded the limit coded into our softswitch, causing a time out and data conflicts.

After we located and fixed the problem, both the customer and the Huawei team were able to breathe a sigh of relief. We couldn't help but laugh that we had wondered about some attack on the satellites. I'm sure the team in charge of the satellites was glad to be cleared of the blame as well.

Today, our softswitch is in service on many customer networks, and we now have better ways to diagnose problems. We don't often have to send engineers halfway around the world, and we don't ask silly questions about satellite attacks.

The Sunspot Mystery

In 2006, a customer in Tibet complained that one of our boards had caused system lockup, so their system had to be rebooted. Before we had figured out the reason, two similar incidents followed within the same month. The customer started to doubt Huawei: "Are your products reliable or not?"

The problem was escalated, and we set up a working group consisting of software and hardware experts dedicated to working out what had gone wrong. We analysed the logs, reviewed the code, and checked the boards and components. After repeated analysis, we found that the issue was caused by bits flipping (binary zeroes changing to ones and ones changing to zeroes). Why did the flipping happen? Was it a software or hardware problem? We had no idea.

In a temporary meeting room less than 10m^2 in size, our software and hardware experts sat thinking hard about the problem. We felt a little frustrated because every idea proved to be a dead end. At the end of the meeting, the colleague responsible for managing the equipment muttered to himself: "Does our equipment suffer from altitude sickness, too?"

"Hey, that could be it!" Our hardware expert, Dalton Du, exclaimed. "Tibet is exposed to high levels of radiation. The rays from sunspots could cause bits to flip in the memory and cache."

Sunspots? It sounded suspiciously like another 'satellites under attack'. Could this speculation be correct?

Everyone was intrigued by the idea. We immediately started to look up the activity curves of sunspots and examples of chip failures caused by radiation. And we found evidence that it did happen. We also studied the number of hours of sunshine over the past few years in Tibet and discovered something interesting: our boards failed at a time when sunspot activity in Tibet was much higher than in previous years.

But how was this possible? Our customer looked incredulous when we suggested this might be the cause. But at Huawei, we are always rigorous about proving our bold ideas. So, in the lab, hundreds of miles away, the platform working group immediately started work on a radiation experiment. They simulated bombardment with high-energy particles and, soon, they managed to reproduce the same bit-flipping effect.

"They've found it!" The testing guys at the frontline waved the test report excitedly. "We should run a longer test and try to find the pattern."

We had found the cause of the problem, but how could we fix it? The best way would be to replace the hardware and use a coating that could block sunspot radiation. But the customer was unwilling to do so, as it was such a big project. So, we had to upgrade the system by adding more memory to create a cache, which could be used to check and write back the data to correct errors. Finally, the board failure was solved.

After that, we invented several patented technologies that enabled us to precisely locate the equipment that had been affected by sunspots in a complex system, and to fix the problems quickly.

Everyone was very excited. We joked that it was not enough for communications engineers to know about communications any more. We had to learn astronomy and geography as well.

From 20 Minutes to 40 Seconds

The success of our first-generation softswitch platform enabled Huawei to seize a leading position in the market. However, the communications industry was growing explosively. In 2007, a competitor planned to launch a new platform based on blade server architecture. Back then, I was in the maintenance department. One day, I received a phone call from my former manager. He said: "Come back and help develop the second-generation platform."

I had watched how our first-generation platform was born and I had a bond with it. I committed myself to the development of the new platform immediately.

The first problem was the selection of software architecture. The product architect argued for using the old architecture. He said: "We can directly migrate our first-generation platform onto the new hardware. This involves less work and will help us launch a more stable platform quickly." However, the platform architect insisted on a new architecture: "If we don't build a new platform, we will not be able to differentiate ourselves from our competitors."

The two sides argued on, and I was very conflicted. Technically, I thought we should select a new architecture but, when it came to delivery, it would be a safer choice to use the old one. After several rounds of review by product-line experts, we decided to use new architecture. We wanted to ensure that our core network products could maintain their leading position for the next five years and would be able to evolve in the future.

However, developing a whole new platform was easier said than done. When commissioning the platform and products, we came across many problems. It was the first time we had used a Linux-based system instead of our own operating system.

The second-generation platform team in 2007

The Linux package was more than 1 gigabyte in size, and it took four to five hours to instal a single board. We had to reboot the system when adding or removing a network card, so the system wasn't plug-and-play, but this feature was what telecom operators wanted. We introduced the industry's leading database to replace our own, but every upgrade and switch took a long time, and there was nothing we could do to shorten it. With the new operation and maintenance (O&M) architecture, a huge volume of logs was required to identify a problem. When the platform was trialled for the first time, the log files were so big that it was quicker to drive them back to the lab in a hard drive than to transmit them.

After the product was delivered and accepted internally, the services team prepared a PowerPoint presentation dozens of pages long, pointing out nearly 100 problems with the platform. They even filed a complaint to the product line. During that period, more than 100 problems were being found in our internal tests every day, and we still had over 1 million lines of code to write. We were like a crippled giant, unable to move forward.

"You have chosen the wrong architecture. You should have used the first-generation architecture." We were drowning in accusations. Under great pressure, Li Huabin, director of the platform department, went to talk with the product teams. He asked them to push back their deadlines and reduce their demands. Finally, the scope and timeline were readjusted. This was the first time that the company's platform department had held such in-depth discussions with product teams, and the closer engagement won us their understanding and support. But they were still dependent on us to deliver, and our customers were waiting. We were determined to turn the situation around.

We started with the Linux operating system. It took 20 minutes to upload it into the communications module, which was unacceptable. We would have to slim the operating system down. Our first attempt failed to achieve the goal – loading the software still took 10 minutes.

But that was unacceptable, as 40 seconds was the maximum possible time allowed. If we couldn't reach the same speeds as the old architecture, customers would not accept the new architecture. So we continued: pre-loading, embedding ... and we shortened the upload time by half, to 5 minutes. It got harder and harder as we continued, so we had to figure out one solution after another, discussed them with systems experts, and tried out every method we could think of. Each time we would cut the upload time second by second.

Finally we made it. We completed the upload of the operating system in 40 seconds while providing many carrier-class features such as a kernel black box, hot swap, and high-precision timer. We had successfully developed our first Linux operating system for the telecom sector. We then worked with suppliers to improve the efficiency of database upgrades and recover the systems in the unlikely event of a crash. In the end, we managed to pass our customers' technical reviews as planned.

We had come through dozens of setbacks and challenges. The second-generation platform was a great success, thanks to the hard work of hundreds of employees over hundreds of days and nights. With its leading technological architecture, the platform has helped our core network products to maintain our technical competitive edge. The platform is now serving over 3 billion users worldwide.

The Secret of Zero Downtime

In 2009, we won a lot of major orders. But one leading telecom operator published a request for proposals with a surprise requirement for reliability: they demanded hitless upgrades. During system upgrades, there should be no interruption of service, and no impact on phone users.

Our first reaction was that this was impossible. A mobile phone or a computer has to be rebooted and all software must be shut down when it is upgraded to a new version. This takes several minutes.

The hitless upgrade team

This operator's requirement was like a computer being updated while a movie was being played on it. I was the director of the design department, and I was under great pressure. I brought together experts from various domains and set up a dedicated hitless upgrade team.

The first solution we came up with was dividing the system into two planes, with the old and the new software versions running concurrently. This meant the software was never completely reset, which allowed us to minimize interruption time. We only needed a single instruction to switch between the two versions, and services were only interrupted during the switchover, a window of less than 10 seconds. To make this solution work, we could not do anything to the old version while it was still running on the network, so we had to set up the partitioning of the two planes in the new version. We isolated the signals, used high-availability partitioning, and with O&M support, we got the two planes to run in parallel without interfering with each other.

But how could we prevent the disconnection of ongoing calls? The only way was to back up all call data on the new version. But the data structures of both versions were always changing. In those thousands or even tens of thousands of data structures, an error in one single byte could easily cause an unrecoverable error. How could we avoid them? Manual comparison? We were drawing a blank.

Then our platform expert, Lin Guoren, suggested that we could apply the rationale of a compiler for data analysis and comparison. I suddenly remembered that we often used this same approach when we were locating network errors. We immediately found books explaining how compilers work, and finally we were able to carry out automatic data comparison.

At the end of 2009, we completed the prototype for the hitless upgrade system in our lab. During system upgrades, all calls remained connected and the delay in establishing new services was kept within 5 seconds. On 7 April 2010, we signed our contract with the customer and made our first breakthrough in North America.

Do We Really Need to Reinvent Ourselves?

In 2011, I became the chief architect of Huawei's core network platform. At that time, cloud computing was emerging in the IT industry, and we were keenly aware that it would have a revolutionary impact on communications technology. However, opinions within the company varied: our second-generation platform remained way ahead of our competitors. Developing a new cloud-based platform would mean a huge investment and risk of failure. Did we really need to reinvent ourselves?

Faced with such a difficult decision, I felt a lot of weight was resting on my shoulders. What should our next step be? Which architecture should we use?

We then started to conduct research on key cloud technologies, such as Kernel-based Virtual Machine (KVM) and OpenStack.

We also worked with other departments and our customers to explore and verify cloud technology.

At the beginning of 2012, we sent a group of experts to Huawei's Sweden Research Center to conduct research on cloud-based platform architecture. In May 2012, at our first meeting with telecom operator V on cloud technology, our vision and architecture for cloud were well received by the customer, and they said they wanted to conduct joint innovation with Huawei. In October that same year, a European standards organization proposed network functions virtualization (NFV), which coincided with our vision for cloud.

At that point, we shifted the focus of our work from technological experimentation to the development of a working version. However, more tough problems were awaiting us: the cutting-edge architecture, cost, performance, and ease of maintenance ... Each one of these areas was a research project in itself. Were we in line with industry trends? Were costs controllable? Would this technology be easy to operate and maintain?

I had a lot of sleepless nights. Sometimes at midnight, I would suddenly come up with a new idea, and I would get up immediately to write it down. After more than 30 meetings with our industry experts and product architects, we finally adopted a multi-layer cloud solution. Along the way, we made several breakthroughs in major solutions and architecture, such as separating the infrastructure and platform layers and automating service provisioning.

In March 2013, we completed the world's first proof of concept for cloud technology with telecom operator V. In October 2014, we built the world's first network with NFV-based architecture. Following that, we won new orders with many leading telecom operators across North America, Europe, and the Middle East. In the new era, we were once again at the top of the industry.

Looking back over the past decade or more, Huawei's tolerance of failure gave us opportunities to learn from our errors.

NFV workshop

Even though we have had some tough failures, we are still as passionate as ever. We always pick ourselves up and find ways to turn around even in the direst situations.

Connecting the World with Wireless

By Lv Jinsong

The other day, I spotted an article that said: "From the wastes of outer Siberia, to the treacherous slopes of Mt. Kilimanjaro; from the heights of 8,000-metre Mt. Everest, to the icy depths of the North and South Poles; from the harshest reaches of Africa, to the luxury malls of Paris, London, and Sydney … wherever you go on this planet, Huawei is there. Every single day, over 2 billion people use networks built by Huawei to call each other, connect, and communicate."

That powerful description captured my attention and set me gradually unfolding all my memories from the time I spent in this company, which stretches back 18 years.

China's Own GSM

At the end of the 1990s, China's mobile communications were evolving from 1G (analog) to 2G (GSM). Chinese equipment manufacturers were rushing to develop their own GSM systems. But overseas telecom giants, such as Ericsson, Nokia, and Motorola, already had mature systems for commercial use. We had a lot of catching up to do.

As the saying goes, fools rush in where angels fear to tread. A brash troupe of Huawei engineers were eager to take on the challenge of building China's own GSM system. Armed with our experience in developing analog communications technology, fewer than 30 R&D engineers launched into what was to be a hard, but joyful, GSM project. We faced huge challenges. To start with, the big Western companies had R&D teams numbering in the hundreds. Our people were going to need some fancy footwork. But we set ourselves the most challenging targets: to have a working model by mid-1997, and to be in production by the end of the same year. At the time, it seemed like a mission impossible. The GSM protocols alone ran to dozens of volumes. We printed them all out and they made a stack several meters high. There were protocols for base stations, base station controllers, core network switches and much more. We had almost no experience in these areas.

I remember that every one of us had a copy of what we called our 'Bible': *Principles of Mobile Communications*. We spent our days in the lab and our nights hitting the books. Lab tests, reading, lab tests, reading … when we came across a problem we couldn't understand, we would ask any specialist we could find, or comb through the literature for an explanation. At the start, we were on the third floor of Building 1 in Shenzhen High-tech Industrial Park. But we had to move several times because there wasn't enough room for us, until we finally found a home in Building 3. By 1998, we had colonized the entire building for wireless R&D. The whole project was electrified by a sense that everyone was giving their utmost to achieve one shared goal. It was a feeling we had never experienced before in the research centres.

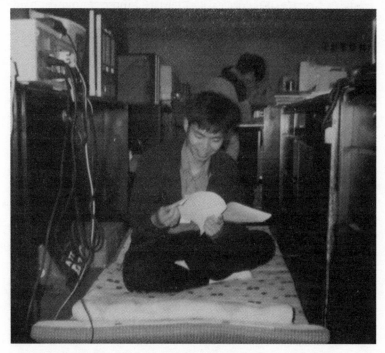

No background, no experience; just passion, youth, and futons

The GSM display at the PT/Expo China, 1997

Our team was growing, and each injection of new blood raised the intensity another notch. The climate in Shenzhen is hot, so we were working stripped down to our vests. We would often spend the night in the labs, wake to splash some water over ourselves in the bathrooms, then get straight back to work. None of us allowed ourselves to be distracted by anything; we all kept our eyes fixed on the task ahead of us. We just wanted to make our system and make it well. Every one of us took on a number of different roles simultaneously. We all knew the equipment back to front, so it was easy to work together. When we looked at the numbers flowing through interface A, we could see immediately which signalling had gone wrong. Sometimes we would be able to guess what had gone wrong, and whose code had the problem, just by monitoring the lab over the LAN in the office.

We spent more than a year frantically developing behind closed doors. Finally, it was 5 September 1997. That evening, everyone gathered in the lab on the east corner of the fourth floor.

Staying on top in the wireless communications industry is like trying to paddle a boat upstream. Every bit of progress you make, you are always in danger of being swept back out to sea.

We were down to the very last process. But, for some reason, it wasn't flowing. Everyone in the team was racking their brain to find a solution, but nothing we tried seemed to have any effect. Suddenly, Pu Gang brought in a fresh pair of eyes. He asked Jiang Tao to come and see if there might just be a problem with the data configuration. As soon as the two of them checked, they found the problem. They fixed it and we booted the system back up to try again. It worked! The signal went through. There was noise on the line and it wasn't clear, but we had made the very first phone call over Huawei's GSM. The whole team was burning with excitement. I don't think anyone got much sleep that night. The next day, the Huawei management team came to the lab to congratulate us on putting through our very first GSM phone call.

In November that year, Huawei unveiled a complete set of GSM at the PT/Expo China (China's International ICT Exhibition and Conference in Beijing). Under the red national flag, with its five stars, we hung up a banner saying, 'China's own GSM'. It was an arresting image. Telecom operators from all over the country, and senior government officials, hustled over to congratulate us. Soon afterwards, Huawei organized an event in the Great Hall of the People to officially launch a complete set of GSM. That marked the official beginning of Huawei's sales of its GSM.

One-Board Innovation

However, staying on top in the wireless communications industry is like trying to paddle a boat upstream. Every bit of progress you make, you are always in danger of being swept back out to sea. GSM became our most important wireless product, but in 2006, we suddenly started to lose orders, and our profits dropped like a stone. The reason was simply that our base stations were too expensive, and our products did not have the functionality or the ease of maintenance required for the high-end market.

The Wireless Network Product Line decided it was time for another revolution. We launched a project and committed ourselves to building a new GSM dual-carrier module that would catapult us to the top of the market. This was another challenging target, particularly for me, the lead systems designer. I had no idea whether it would actually be possible. But I knew that if we did not try, then we were doomed. If we committed to it, then at least we had a chance of surviving.

At the time, all GSM equipment was sold as a series of separate, modular boards. That is to say, when an operator wanted to build a base station, they needed to set up a cabinet, then slot in a whole assembly of boards: power module, amplifier, wave filter, etc. No equipment manufacturer had the capacity to integrate all of the different modules and still maintain acceptable levels of performance.

So, how were we to make our GSM equipment more competitive? Over many rounds of debate, the Wireless Network Product Line gradually came to a consensus: we would have to do something outside the box. Just improving and upgrading conventional products within the existing architecture wasn't going to be enough. We had to make a new architecture. And we would use the deficiencies of the current equipment to guide us.

Our principle for reshaping the GSM architecture was simplicity: "Simplicity is our competitive edge." We realized that to achieve our goal, we would have to streamline every circuit, strip away every feature that wasn't delivering value to the customer, slim ourselves down and then pare ourselves even finer. So, we gave ourselves the audacious goal of putting everything on just one board. We were going to turn an equipment cabinet into a single circuit board.

It was a seductive vision. But reality was itching to pour cold water on our dreams. How could we possibly make the 'single board' a reality? The answer was by making it simpler, and simpler, and simpler, again. Wherever it was possible to use just one resistor, we banned ourselves from using two. Any functions that could be combined, were combined. Any features that could be eliminated were ruthlessly stripped out. This process of slimming, trimming, and combining sucked most of the redundancy out of the boards. Then it was time to miniaturize: the amplifier, then the power module. Finally, with each module now as simple and small as it could be (using the technology of the day), we were able to piece them together on a single circuit board. We had achieved the single board vision.

The new dual-carrier base station in 2007,
which revitalized Huawei's GSM product line

Now, when customers opened up a cabinet, instead of the mess of boards that they used to see, they saw just a single board, luxuriating in acres of space. Naturally, they were delighted, and the dual carrier module became Wireless Network's first ¥20billion product in terms of profits. In fact, it was this product that finally won us entry to the coveted provincial capital city/direct-controlled municipality networks, and contracts with O2 in Germany. Our Wireless Network Product Line thus completed the long trek from the villages into the heart of the modern metropolis.

Jewel in the Crown

But we were not about to rest on our laurels. Quite the contrary, having tasted success, we were more determined than ever to deliver world-class products.

At the time, GSM multi-carrier technology was widely recognized in the industry as a 'hard nut to crack'. Up until 2007, all GSM systems around the world were limited to the use of single carrier waves. The problem with single carrier is that when the signal switches from one carrier to another, you need a second module to handle the new carrier during switchover. This takes up more space in the cabinet, draws more power, and so on, so it represented a major additional cost for telecom operators. So, virtually every organization out there, from operators, to equipment manufacturers, to universities, to research institutions, wanted to produce a multi-carrier GSM system. But, as yet, the key had eluded everyone.

Before we officially initiated our own GSM multi-carrier R&D project, we spent a few weeks going over and over the GSM protocols and the various technical proposals. As I read through the protocol specifications and looked at the level of experience and expertise in our team, I was not optimistic about our chances. "At best, we've got a 1% chance of managing this," I thought. But, despite the challenges, the Wireless Network Product Line committed itself to redefining the 2G technology market and placing ourselves out in front. In mid-2006, we launched ourselves into a GSM multi-carrier project. I was put in charge of the project, and I started out by taking Tang, Zhu, Deng, and our experts in the Russia research centre through a research of GSM multi-carrier technology.

As I had expected, we quickly ran into difficulties. The challenges were so big that there didn't seem to be anywhere to begin. The technology didn't seem like it would ever fit together and, because we were moving into uncharted territory, there were no models to which we could usefully refer.

We started revising our approach, shifting from a single drive at the target to a more phased approach. We would treat it like an Everest ascent, climbing from camp to camp. In the first phase, we would try with limited bandwidth, to get the principle working; in the second phase, we would expand the bandwidth; in the third phase, we would build a working module and run full-system tests. Once we had some interim targets worked out, we were able to start knocking them down one by one. And not much more than six months later, we were starting to see light at the end of the tunnel, where before there had been none. However, serious problems were lying in wait for us.

To this day, I still shudder at the memory of the grinding difficulty of capturing those last 10 decibels (dB) of gain.

We had spent many, many long nights in the lab testing and trying out ideas to get to our target of 70dB. We were within 10dB of that goal, but then the intermodulation indices had jammed and would not advance another inch, no matter what we did. The closer we got, the harder it was to make progress, and the difficulty was rising exponentially. That was the way intermodulation worked. What none of us expected was that closing this final gap would hold us up for four months. Every day we would run through the process in the lab, and every day we would get no further. At night, we would go home and think about what we could try the next day. Eventually, a glimmer of an idea would come, and we would return to the lab full of hope in the morning, only for the same process to play out, again and again. This was how we spent every day of those four months. Wen, who designed our amplifiers, eventually burst out, "At least in my other projects there were some highs and lows. In this project it's just one long low! Either the numbers don't even flicker, or they tick up once, and then we can never repeat it."

The lack of progress was starting to weigh on the team's confidence. It was a gruelling test of our psychological endurance. "We can't go on like this," everyone started to think. I was losing confidence, too. But, as the leader of the project, I couldn't let anyone see that it was getting to me. So, I stayed brief and to the point: "Let's give it one more go. What schemes have we not tried yet?" Zhu Erni, the product development representative on the project team, was an enthusiastic young man, and he would often say, "Just think of Thomas Edison! Didn't he try over 1,000 materials before he invented the electric light? Everyone laughed at him, but he said that at the very least he'd shown that those 1,000 materials didn't work." And, at that, everyone would straighten up a little and head back in for another look at the theory books, and another look at the data. We would adjust our forward link, adjust our reverse link, tweak the amplifier, and slot the board back into the test rig. We would adapt the algorithms and try them again. We would find the differences in failure data and compare them with past results, to work out which data points were impacting our ultimate indices.

One night in July 2007, fate finally opened a door for us persistent and sometimes stubborn engineers. In a lab filled with amplifier boards, the spectrum analyser finally showed us the result we had been dreaming of. We swapped in another board for testing, then another. Each board gave us the same positive result. But the strongest feeling I had at that moment was more relief than excitement. A year ago, no one had dreamed that this day would happen. We did not cheer or celebrate, because my team and I had exhausted all of our energy. We were like empty husks.

Multi-carrier GSM was a world-class technology. That breakthrough gave us a foothold at the very forefront of the industry. What we did not know then was that it would continue to power Huawei's success long into the future. Multi-carrier GSM laid the critical technological foundations for the SingleRAN solution, which would take the world by storm a few years later. It was a contribution not just to our wireless network business, but to the mobile communications industry as a whole.

From Follower to Leader, Step by Step

The successful development of GSM multi-carrier technology was like seizing the jewel in the crown. It brought us much joy and excitement but, at the same time, being an industry leader presented us with bigger challenges and confusion. We faced the question of how to develop our next technology plan.

The multi-carrier GSM project team

Spectrum is the most valuable resource in wireless communications. The entire wireless communications industry is always looking for higher spectrum efficiency. We are always trying to transmit more data using less spectrum resources. Telecom operators struggle to offer the largest capacity for traffic using the simplest and most compact devices. Over years of debate between the Wireless Network Red Team and Blue Team, we gradually defined a leading 4M strategy. 4M means: multi-carrier, multi-RAT, MIMO, and multi-band technologies. Multi-carrier means exploiting multiple carrier waves, all using the same standard; multi-RAT means converging multiple different standards (also known as multi-mode technology, including 2G/3G/4G); MIMO (multiple-input and multiple-output) means using multiple transmit and receive antennas; and multi-band means using multiple spectrum segments to realize broadband speeds. These four key technologies allow telecom operators to maximize their spectrum efficiency, whether they use single or multi-standard technology.

In 2007, we had made a breakthrough in the first 'M' with the GSM multi-carrier technology. Huawei's multi-carrier transmission significantly improved GSM's spectrum efficiency. Over rounds of debate, we bounced ideas off each other, and finally developed a simple and disruptive proposal for the second 'M': Support 2G, 3G, and 4G in a single hardware module. We would offer operators a full palette and allow them to choose whatever colour they liked (that is, whatever technology standard they wanted to use). As we researched this second 'M', we discovered a rare market opportunity. At that time, some European operators were restructuring their GSM networks, and they asked Huawei to provide a solution for a 900MHz frequency band network. This network would support 2G initially, and then be upgraded to 3G by software. We had the technology ready ahead of the customer request and had made the key breakthroughs in GSM multi-carrier technology. The Wireless Network Product Line pounced on this new market and launched a big wireless strategy – SingleRAN. It was the perfect moment, and we saw a leapfrog development in our wireless products and solutions in the following years.

In 2011, we built a remote radio unit (RRU) with the highest bandwidth, smallest size, and highest efficiency in the world. This was our third 'M', and it made us a world leader in both software and hardware. Finally, in 2014, we set up the multi-band broadband platform, supporting the fourth 'M'. This platform solved a major pain point for operators: the proliferation of antennas and hardware. It enabled convergence of both networks and different bands. Once again, it was a world first.

The path from 1M to 4M was not just a numerical advance. These seemingly obscure technical terms describe the simplest possible philosophy: every effort is made to gather together the cat's cradle of threads that make up wireless communications technology, so that we can maximize spectrum efficiency and serve the deep need that people have for free communications.

Opening of the 4.5G Industry Summit

Communication Across the Planet

Looking back over the 18 years I have spent in the Wireless Network Product Line, we have made tenacious explorations and significant technological breakthroughs, ranging from our first GSM phone call to the Dual Density TRX Unit (DTRU), and from multi-carrier technology to the SingleRAN solution. Our work may not be well known to most people, but we have been playing a big role in your everyday communications when you make a phone call to your family far away, video chat with your spouse, or share a photo of your child on WeChat. Our work makes the world a global village and breaks down the communication boundaries between people.

Now, we are in the middle of the second decade of the 21st century. Human society keeps on progressing, driven by emerging technologies like 5G, big data, smart devices, higher-level machine learning, the internet of things, virtual reality and augmented reality, cloud computing, and smart everything.

People are desperate to break down the barriers of distance and build connections between things. It has been a long and arduous journey, but I am convinced that, with our insights into the future, our understanding of customer needs, and Huawei's daring and innovative spirit, we will realize our dream of communication across the planet through the decades ahead.

Revolutionizing the Telephone Line

By Li Dong

In the early 1980s, I had a fixed-line phone at home. To make a phone call, I had to pick up the phone, dial the operator, and tell them which number I wanted to call. After that, I had to wait for a while before being connected. As a child, the telephone was quite a mystery to me. I was always itching to take it apart and see what was inside.

Unexpectedly, after graduating from university, I took a job working with telephones. This has helped me uncover the mystery of the telephone. I would even go so far as to call it fate.

An Early Dream

In 1999, I joined Huawei's switch product line. According to my mentor, "At Huawei, you are working with a group of engineers of vision."

I asked my mentor what his vision was. He replied that in the early 1990s, China's communications equipment market had been dominated by overseas manufacturers, such as Nortel Networks (Canada's leading telecommunications equipment provider), Siemens, Fujitsu, and Alcatel. At the time, a fixed-line phone would cost thousands of yuan, which was quite a burden for most families. Huawei therefore set a goal at its inception: first to develop its own communications equipment, then to sell it into overseas markets so as to provide high-quality communications services for people all over the world. His words filled me with inspiration and enthusiasm, and I felt like I was joining a great and glorious team.

It was a great vision. But reality was ready to pour cold water on our dreams.

The Case of the Mysterious Rats

We had no experience or background. We had no one to tell us how to do the work. All we had was passion, faith and, of course, growing pains.

I remember one time when the subscriber line boards burned out and were damaged. The sales team complained about it and instructed the R&D team to resolve the problem as soon as possible. First, we had to identify the underlying cause. So, we tried various power failure scenarios, but failed to replicate the problem. After many rounds of tests, we still had no clue what the root cause was.

One team member proposed taking the equipment running on the existing network back to the office to test it. After repeated checks, we discovered that there were water marks on the board. We bounced ideas off each other: communications equipment was not like an air conditioner, so why were water marks on it? Did rats sneak into the equipment room and urinate on the board?

But this was merely an assumption. To verify our assumption and replicate the scenario, we tried sprinkling water on the boards, but failed to achieve a result. We then began thinking: where could we find a rat to test our theory? As we were discussing the issue, my mentor left the office for some time and then came back with a small bottle of yellow liquid – rat urine. I was extremely impressed that he had managed to catch a rat in such a short time. We poured some of it on to the board, and the board immediately started blazing and cracking. We had finally managed to replicate the fire scenario, and were filled with excitement as we gathered around to view the ignition point on the board, even if it smelled bad.

The incident got us thinking: Why would rats urinate on our communications equipment? What were the conditions like where our equipment was actually in use?

To find answers, our maintenance team visited equipment rooms all over the country, only to find that the environments our equipment faced were much worse than we had imagined.

In cities, there were designated equipment rooms for communications equipment. However, in rural areas, equipment was stored close to grain and quilts in shabby cottages, or near hog lots. In southern cities, there was no central heating in winter, and the heated equipment rooms naturally became five-star hotels for

These days, Huawei's equipment can endure a variety of extreme conditions, from deserts to high altitudes, and from frigid cold to intense heat. It can even survive being soaked in water for a long time.

small animals. It was, therefore, not surprising that rats would sleep and urinate in the equipment rooms.

In addition to rats, there were other threats. For instance, an equipment room in Anhui province was left unattended for so long that birds built nests inside; in Guangxi province, where it rains for most of the year, equipment rooms were often damp, and one had 10cm of thick mud on the floor; in the Northeast, our equipment rooms were buried by blizzards.

In those days, our R&D team was constantly visiting customers and solving problems. These days, Huawei's equipment can endure a variety of extreme conditions, from deserts to high altitudes, and from frigid cold to intense heat. It can even survive being soaked in water for a long time. Our equipment, as an old saying goes, can "survive the thinnest air of the upper atmosphere, and the crushing pressure of the deepest depths."

The Hungarian photographer Robert Capa once said, "If your photographs aren't good enough, you're not close enough." We learned from the case of mysterious rat urine that we should always move close enough to customers to understand the real situation.

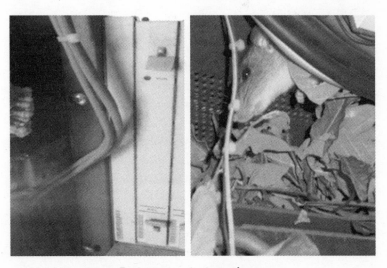

Equipment rooms in rural areas

Thunder Close Enough to Touch

When I was young, I knew not to watch television during thunderstorms. Televisions receive signals from rooftop antennas and, during thunderstorms, TVs can easily be destroyed by lightning.

It is the same for our communications equipment. Subscriber line boards are connected to hundreds of thousands of pairs of outgoing telephone lines and are vulnerable to lightning strikes. To test the vulnerability of subscriber line boards, we used to place equipment out on the networks. We created a nationwide map of stormy regions and we would install our boards there at the start of the rainy season, and wait for lightning to strike. However, this method took a long time. It didn't exactly support the fast pace of verification and improvement.

The equipment breakdowns due to thunderstorms frustrated us. Once, Hang Jiong, who managed the maintenance of our network, sent us an email: "I have been a maintenance manager for quite a long time, and I can understand the needs of our field teams and our customers. Their networks are frequently interrupted, and systems can break down at any time. User complaints are flooding in. We cannot afford to let this situation continue for even one more day."

One day when I was driving home, I heard a rainstorm alert over the radio. It suddenly occurred to me that we could simulate a thunderstorm to perform testing instead of merely waiting for storms.

So, we began to look for equipment to simulate thunderstorms. When we were developing a new subscriber line board, we found a manufacturer who could build us customized generators that were powerful enough to recreate the voltages in lightning strikes. We installed a few generators in the lab and performed hundreds of simulations on every version of our hardware, trying to figure out how failures might occur.

In 2001, Huawei started shipping subscriber boards in scale to telecoms operator China Tietong, serving 2 million of their customers that same year. When I visited the production line and saw hundreds of boards passing by one after another, I was filled with pride and excitement. However, at the same time I was worried about reliability problems. But the company's statistics showed a significant decline in returns due to failures caused by lightning.

Broadband Golden Age: Not Built in a Day

In 2003, we crossed into broadband's golden age. There was a big shift in the focus of construction from voice networks to DSL broadband networks. We wondered whether we could use a single board to provide access to both the broadband and voice networks. That was how the Combo board came into being, and it soon became the ace in the hole of Huawei's access products. We thought that the Combo board's development was completed but, on the contrary, we had only taken the first step along an arduous road ahead.

By the end of 2004, a new challenge had emerged. British Telecom (BT) wanted to build a '21st Century Network' that worked entirely on an all-IP architecture. To meet their needs, we could use our integrated access device UA5000 to support the Combo board, but we would have to double the board's density without expanding its size. It seemed like a mission impossible.

The company saw this as a great opportunity, and Wu Haining from marketing accepted BT's request immediately. I can still remember on the morning before I returned to China from the UK, I was wandering a park in Ipswich (the town in which BT is headquartered), trying to figure out how I could explain to my team members that we had taken up such a huge task.

But there was no turning back. All we could do was start with the target capacity – a 32-line Combo board. We realized we would have to use the very highest capacity chipsets available in the industry.

We had a tight schedule, so we often had to stay up late into the night and return home in the early hours. Zhou Jinlin, our department director, worked with us deep into the night, and used to drive us home. A new team member, Sun Jiangang, lived far away from the company, so he would often make up a bed in the office and begin working early in the morning. We tried to persuade him to go back home to sleep, but he said he didn't want to waste time travelling back and forth, and that he could only sleep easy after finishing all his work.

The project was much more difficult than we had expected. In the middle of the project, we discovered that our high-density chipsets did not have enough memory. If we started all over again, we would lose control of the entire project and not be able to meet the deadline. Just as we were wondering what to do, someone suggested that, when we run out of memory, we just overwrite the software code. When the chipset needed the code again, it could just download it from the board software. While this solution worked, new problems arose. The single-chip microcomputer had quite a slow download speed, and it took nearly ten minutes to download the full code. This was not acceptable.

I called in an expert specializing in board software, and asked him to restructure the code from the bottom up. It was an out-of-the-blue request, but he agreed. We have a saying: "Huawei people never say no." The software expert was very efficient. He came to me two days later, telling me it now only took two minutes to download the software. But two minutes was still too long. After a few more days, he reduced the download time down to one minute. I felt terrible, but I still pushed him for more time reductions. Finally, he managed to cut the download time to less than four seconds. It is amazing, what Huawei colleagues will do for you. I was moved by such commitment.

The Sword of Damocles

BT had extremely strict standards on product reliability. Their request for a tender specified that if total annual downtime was more than five minutes, Huawei would face serious penalties. This clause hung over our heads like the Sword of Damocles.

I remember one day in 2005, we were doing a final hardware check before populating boards. Together with Xiao Ruijie, Project Leader of the UA5000 line card hardware development team, we went through more than 40 risk issues one by one. Where we could eliminate them, we did. Those we couldn't eliminate, we had to accept as a risk. By the time we had worked through every one of those issues, the sun was nearly up. I then had breakfast with Zhou Jinlin, but I wasn't comfortable leaving us open to so many risks. Zhou saw that I was unsettled, and said, "Don't worry about it. The sun will still rise, whatever happens."

This was how we kept each other going, and that was how a group of young telecom rookies came to instal the world's highest density combo cards and help the company take its first crucial step as a BT supplier. Huawei finally got itself off the bench and into BT's starting lineup. We started delivering stable fixed-line broadband services to tens of millions of UK users.

One day in 2015, I was reading a weekly project update from a colleague in the UK, when I spotted a reference to the UA5000. That was the board we had installed back in 2005, and it was now being phased out in favour of our next-generation MA5600T. All of a sudden, the weight that had been on my shoulders ten years ago was suddenly lifted: our equipment had made it. That day, I took some colleagues out for a buffet lunch. It was a reward – and perhaps compensation – for the pressure I'd taken on myself.

Copper Wires Can Survive for Another Century

The internet is traditionally accessed via phone lines. Due to low speeds, in recent years people have been pushing to replace copper wire cables with fibre optic cables.

But that's easier said than done. Optical fibre is very cost-effective, but what operators are most concerned about is the deployment of fibre, especially the last mile.

In many European countries, laying fibre means digging trenches through beautiful gardens or drilling holes in the walls of protected ancient castles. It is quite costly and time-consuming, and in some places there is just no way to do it. In many places around the world, customers refuse to allow phone companies in to lay fibre, as they might damage the property. If we could increase the transmission speed over existing copper wire networks up to the level of fibre, it would become the most economical and fastest way to access the internet.

Since 2011, Huawei has been investing in the development of copper wire vectoring, trying to increase the transmission speed of copper telephone lines to 100 Mbit/s. This was still in the theoretical research stage, and Huawei had only just finished developing its own vectoring algorithms. When we tried to translate those algorithms into a product, we experienced the huge gap between theory and reality. To complete hundreds of millions of computing requests within five microseconds, we employed the industry-leading field-programmable gate array (FPGA) chipsets. But the power demands far exceeded our system parameters.

The R&D process was more difficult than anything we had ever tried before. We were constantly improving the product design to make reductions of nanoseconds or to shave off a few milliwatts of power. At the same time, the sales teams were putting immense pressure on us to give them a product they could show to customers. The project team felt overwhelmed. We had been given another seemingly impossible task. But I remember a line from a Chinese TV show called *Drawing Sword*, which was set during World War II. The character Li Yunlong looks at the city gates and declares, "Those gates are a tough bit of bone, all right. But I'm going to bite through them before the enemy reinforcements arrive, even if I break my teeth doing it." I joked with the project manager responsible for chipsets, "If we cannot develop the product, we should simply have a fight and let the company fire us both. It would be a relief for us, and it would give the R&D team a way out without losing face."

But where there's a will, there's a way. We Huawei people cannot be easily defeated. The R&D team never stopped struggling

The R&D process was more difficult than anything we had ever tried before. We were constantly improving the product design to make reductions of nanoseconds or to shave off a few milliwatts of power.

forward. We faced many difficulties, one after another, and suffered innumerable setbacks. Finally, one evening before the Spring Festival, we uploaded the latest compiled software into the system and began testing. We held our breath as we waited for the results, and we began to see rows of lights on the modem starting to blink regularly in the darkness. Zhang Jian, the project manager, was controlling the back-end system, and he shouted suddenly, "It's up! It's up!" We rushed to his computer and saw the activity at the vectoring port soar above 100 Mbit/s, up to the theoretical maximum. The entire lab was soon filled with cheers, and we high-fived each other excitedly.

Over the next few months, we experienced setbacks and made breakthroughs, and our new product gradually found the right track. Finally in 2012, our vectoring product had the best performance and largest capacity in the industry, and won orders for use in several national broadband projects from key customers, including Swisscom, BT, and Eircom. In October 2012, our vectoring product VDSL won the Best Broadband Equipment Award from the Broadband World Forum for its high capacity.

The vectoring R&D team with the Swisscom technology innovation team in 2012

Due to our technological breakthroughs, we managed to change the push for 'fibre instead of copper' into 'fibre plus copper'. Huawei had announced to the world that now people in old European castles can also surf the internet anytime they want, and that copper wires will not be out of date for at least a century.

In Switzerland, Huawei Is the Fairy Godmother

Technology fanatics are always ready to take on a challenge. It's hard, but joyful. Just as we made breakthroughs to enable 100 Mbit/s on copper wire, we were now shooting for gigabit broadband speeds. Under the leadership of Dr Long Guozhu, a Huawei Fellow who specialized in copper lines, the research team made a series of technical discoveries over the course of a year. In 2011, we developed our own gigabit prototype and demonstrated Gbit/s speeds over short distances in a pair of copper wires.

European operators showed great interest in this prototype. Swisscom established a showcase in Riggisberg, central Switzerland, and invited regulators and governments from other European countries to visit. This prototype completely changed major operators' understanding of the bandwidth potential of copper wires. In later meetings of the International Telecommunication Union (ITU), key technologies based on Huawei's prototype defined a new copper wire access standard, called G.fast.

Huawei equipment in manholes in Switzerland

But next was product development and it would bring many more challenges. In Switzerland, in order to get our equipment close enough to end users, we had to lay copper cables in the underground pipes of Switzerland's towns and villages. When spring came and the snow melted, the water would flow into the pipe shafts and our equipment would be soaked for several weeks. How could we ensure our equipment would continue to work stably for at least two decades under such extreme conditions?

In early 2013, we travelled to Switzerland to examine the installation environment. One manhole was located in the grassland at the foot of a mountain. When I jumped into the manhole to check the installation environment, a cow leaned over, looking down at me, shaking its head with a seemingly scornful look. The bell hanging beneath its neck rang, as if the cow was asking me, "Are you sure you want to do this?"

In 2015, after two years' efforts, we helped Swisscom win the world's first G.fast users in Bibern, a beautiful small town in northern Switzerland. Bibern is surrounded by hills, forests, rivers, and lakes. More than 200 households live there, enjoying the tranquility of nature. However, they had virtually no mobile signal in their valley, and their broadband speed was far from satisfying.

With our new copper wire gigabit technology, we helped Swisscom deploy ultra-high-definition television services in Bibern and proved that the speed of copper wires could compare with that of optical fibres. During the launch event, local residents shook my colleagues' hands and repeatedly expressed their thanks. Markus E. Eberhard, vice president of Swisscom, presented certificates to residents for being the world's first G.fast users and said, "I'd like to express my special thanks to Huawei. You've done a great job. Through your ongoing efforts under huge pressure, and your constant improvements to this solution, we can now stand here at the launch of Swisscom G.fast, showcasing the next generation of broadband to the world."

On that day, my colleague, Vivian Gong, also felt deeply moved. "There are some people and some things in the world that

Swisscom presented certificates to the world's first G.fast users

make you so happy that you could cry. It's like finding a fairy godmother. It's a pleasure to deliver services to them," she said.

Looking back on my past 18 years at Huawei, we have moved from telephone lines and narrowband voice to megabit ADSL networks, and then from vectoring VDSL to G.fast with giga-bit-level speeds. We are committed to enriching people's lives through communication. We have helped the company achieve business success and, at the same time, we have personally ben-efited. Looking back at how big our ambitions were at the begin-ning, it makes me think of the words to a song: "Those dreams we had, we held them so tight. Now we've reached the top, it finally feels right."

Huawei Antennas: Survive and Thrive

By Zhou Taoyuan

In August 2010, I was promoted to director of the Antenna Business Unit. It was an enormous challenge for me.

The Antenna Business Unit had not been performing as it should and had been restructured several times over the previous three years in response to quality issues. Customer satisfaction was low, and we had become a joke among the sales teams. "If you value your life," they said, "don't get mixed up in antenna sales." When a Huawei antenna developed a fault, it didn't just mean extra work for them, it was a reputation issue that affected all Huawei products. At a strategy meeting, the company leadership gave us an ultimatum: "Sort yourselves out within the next three years, or we are shutting down the unit."

We had our backs to the wall. It was do or die. So, we set out to prove that we could do it.

A Huawei Single Antenna in Amsterdam

The Decision to Go 'Single'

We realized that we had missed the boat on 3G, and we could not let that happen again on 4G. By 2010, telecom operators were already starting to build their LTE (that is, 4G) networks. Our competitors were already developing tri-band antennas to meet operator demand. How could we steal a march on them? If we just followed the same path as everyone else, we would always be two steps behind. We needed something new, something different, to give our products the edge.

It was just at that time that the Wireless team introduced the 'five-band, three-mode' SingleRAN solution. That meant we would have to converge multiple antennas into a single unit that could handle multiple frequency bands simultaneously. So, we set ourselves a target: by 2013, we would develop a five-band, three-mode antenna. It would support the 800 MHz, 900 MHz, 1,800 MHz, 2,100 MHz, and 2,600 MHz bands, and GSM, UMTS, and LTE specifications.

No Compromises

Work officially began on the Single Antenna project in September 2011. If you liken a single-band antenna to the source of a river, our multi-band antenna was like an entire watershed: multiple tributaries (signals) combining together into a single flow, which then streams out into the great ocean of the network.

The difficulty of the development process rises exponentially with the number of bands you want to include on a single antenna and, for this project, the design constraints were formidable. We developed two initial ideas. One was simply to stack the different bands, one on top of the other. This would be quick to develop, but we would lose some performance. The other was to divide the antenna horizontally. This would give us performance comparable to using separate single-band antennas, but it would increase the size of the unit. That would be a negative when it came to installation.

I wasn't satisfied with either of these two approaches, because they didn't respond to what we were hearing from our customers. Every customer was telling us the same thing: they wanted no drop-off in performance and no additional difficulty in installation. We ultimately all agreed: we would make no trade-offs or compromises in our design. We had to find a better structure for our single antenna. It had to have more bands, with no reduction in performance and no increase in size; it had to have more ports with no extra weight.

The engineering team went back to the drawing board, and they came up with a new approach: side-by-side (SBS). This meant a complex pattern of dipoles (receivers) spread across the face of the antenna. It allowed our many tributaries – signals on different frequency bands – multiple points of access to the main channel, and maximized the flow of information. It was a bold stroke of engineering.

In November 2011, I gave the go-ahead for the first leg of our development process. I put Kevin Xiao, who was head of the Architecture Design Department, in charge of the development team. I told them to give us an answer in three months: was the SBS design really feasible?

When we built new single-band antennas, we generally moved directly to the prototype phase, because we had a lot of experience. But for this multi-band technology, we would need to run network simulations first. Xiao got in touch with two of the engineers in the Performance Department: Dr Zhang and Nix. Dr Zhang had a team in Shanghai, and Nix had a team in Xi'an. Our Shenzhen facility was not set up with a large simulator back then, so we had to output all the parameters of our antenna design, then send them off to Shanghai and Xi'an to be run through the simulator. It took a week to run a full simulation, and every time we tweaked a single parameter, we had to run the whole simulation over again.

It was a time-consuming process and demanded great patience from all of us. Every detail had to be talked through, checked, and rechecked. Xiao spent his weeks flying between the three locations, spending a few days in each. After three months of this, the team had collected ten sets of comprehensive simulation data. The Shanghai results and the Xi'an results matched perfectly, and the feasibility of the SBS design had been officially demonstrated. Performance was 15% better than a vertical stacked solution, and the width and weight of the unit were within the specified ranges, so they would not cause any additional difficulty during installation. It looked like the rest of the process should be plain sailing.

Don't Listen to the Doubters

When designing antennas, it is vital to minimize passive intermodulation (PIM) – the interference caused by multiple signals hitting a complex receiver or surface. The amount of interference allowed is so small, it is like one planet Earth crashing into another planet Earth, and kicking up no more than a bean-sized bit of debris. Back in the 20th century, NASA discovered that in satellite communications, almost any metal connection or surface will create intermodulation, because of the way different parts respond to the incoming signal. It could be a different metal, different coating, or even slightly different levels of oxidation or precision in the tooling; it could be variation in the pressure between contacts, in current, or in frequency. Temperature, humidity, and many other factors, which we cannot possibly control, can all play a role in creating PIM.

The ability to control PIM has long been recognized as the key to success in antenna manufacturing, and it is an area in which some of Huawei's competitors maintained a clear lead for many years. Our multi-band antenna was inevitably going to be more complex than a single-band antenna, with more connections and more parts, so potential sources of PIM were everywhere. Any tiny imperfection could generate interference and degrade our signal. We had to find a solution.

The man to take on this task was an engineer named Gorden Guo. The first thing he did was take a faulty antenna out, bash it around some more, then conduct every kind of test and experiment he could. He collected a lot of data and was able to find the patterns, but that didn't tell him exactly what the cause of the problems was.

Guo was reading a book at the time on intermodulation in satellite communications, and he realized that a lot of the theories in the book could be applied to our work. He decided to take a trip to the University of Valencia in Spain, where the author lived, to spend a day talking to him. This meeting was a huge success, and the ideas they produced laid the foundation for the rest of our work.

Now the hard work started and we went at it around the clock. Bolts are one of the most important factors affecting PIM. In an antenna, bolts are not just part of the supporting structure, they act as functional signal channels themselves. As we were looking into the correct levels of torque for our bolts, we ran into a whole series of issues. Could the tightening of bolts cause deformation in the connections and the structural elements? Might it cause creep over time? How could we ensure that bolt tightness remained constant over the lifetime of the product? What kind of tool could deliver torque with the levels of precision that we needed? How could we test the PIM effects of different kinds of contact between different metals? What could we do when no test tools for these issues were commercially available?

Many people thought that Huawei simply didn't have the ability to solve the problems of PIM, but Guo refused to listen to the doubters. He and his team built their own test devices – creating a number of new patents and proprietary technologies along the way. However, all this additional work was leaving us far behind our original product development schedule.

Closed-shop development was never going to be fast enough. We had to follow the advice of our founder, Ren Zhengfei, and "absorb the energy of the universe over a cup of coffee". That means getting

A boat on a little river can sail serenely on, but in the turbulence of a multi-river system, there is always the danger of capsizing.

out there and drawing on the knowledge of the wider community. So, we got in partners to help us with every stage of the process. Industry experts, international PIM research bodies, suppliers of materials, and testing services. They all supported our efforts in engineering, materials selection, testing, and manufacturing processes. Gradually, we chipped away at the problems from all angles. We got in an international soldering expert, Dr Armin Rahn, to work with us for three years to make sure we understood how soldering can affect PIM. No technical detail escaped our notice. Over this long period of concentrated effort, often around the clock, we together solved innumerable technical puzzles.

What Goes into a Wire?

As I said, a single-band antenna is like a single river. A multi-band antenna is many tributaries coming together. The currents form whirlpools, eddies, and undertows. A boat on a little river can sail serenely on, but in the turbulence of a multi-river system, there is always the danger of capsizing.

The kind of cables that we used in single-band antennas caused massive interference in our multi-band Single Antenna system. The slightest movement or flexing of a cable inside the antenna would create noise or cut off user calls altogether.

Electromagnetic interference between antenna cables (sometimes called crosstalk) is a complex issue involving both materials science and electromagnetic theory. There are not many researchers in the world with a thorough knowledge of the issues involved. Our cabling and shielding experts ran simulations of the electromagnetic environment inside the antenna and carefully analysed the cables we were using. Finally, they recommended that we need better shielding on the cables. We researched two-layer shielding, three-layer shielding, and even more layers. These efforts went on for months, but we were still getting interference inside the antenna. We couldn't get the results we needed.

One day we were having a birthday party in the department and, as we cut the cake, one of our wire connection engineers, named Fang, started taking an unusual interest in the structure of the cake: layer upon layer of cream and sponge, all stuck together in a single unit, with fruit blended throughout. It made him think of the multi-layer shielding on our cables. Why couldn't those multiple layers be collapsed into one thin, complex layer? He put down his cake and asked several team members to run straight over to our cable supplier to get started on a new round of engineering, prototyping and testing. The prototype exceeded all of our expectations, and we quickly ordered an entire batch of the new model.

But, when we put our new cables in the antennas, we found that half of the antennas still had levels of crosstalk higher than our quality parameters would allow. Fang set off back to the supplier to see if he could work out what the issue was. It turned out that during mass production, they were careless in the way they cut the wire, and the shielding had split. This was the cause of our stray interference.

It was nearly time for Chinese New Year, so everyone quickly headed over to the supplier to help them sort out the issues before the holiday began. We went through every step of their production process, telling them how to make it better: a new tool specifically to cut our cable, to reduce splitting in the shielding layer; a new layout to prevent metallic dust particles from contaminating our cables. Within two months, we were able to cut down crosstalk to zero.

Over nine months, we iterated and verified eight wiring plans; optimized 18 different versions; finalized and formalized 14 manufacturing processes; and applied for two new patents and two utility models.

Staying One Step Ahead Isn't Easy

In early 2012, I noticed some blistering on the coating of antennas that had been sent back to us for replacement. I went to find Dr Hu, who had worked on materials for more than 30 years. He said that mild blistering like that would not affect the integrity of the aluminum alloy during the lifetime of the antenna, so the components inside would not be affected. But, it was still worth solving the issue, to ensure the quality and strength of the product, and to dispel any doubts in the mind of the customer.

To make our product sturdier, we decided to develop a solution that would resist all types of weather and could be used in any situation. Our materials scientists immersed themselves in investigations of different environments and anti-corrosion manufacturing processes. In 2010, they had started on-site surveys, looking at how corrosion affected our products in use.

From the freezing north of Russia and Finland to the heat of Nigeria; from humid Singapore and Malaysia to the dry dust of Egypt and Kuwait; from the salty air of Peru and islands such as Sri Lanka to the sulfurous climate of the oil-producing Arab countries ... over the course of two years, our materials scientists trekked through more than 30 countries and collected data on over 2,000 base stations. They analysed dew condensation and depth of snow, air conditioner exhausts, and chemical plant smoke and runoff, to see how each would affect the type and rate of corrosion. They even looked at bird droppings and ant saliva. We also set up a test station at the very saltiest point on the island of Hainan, and placed several products there so that we could track how they were affected.

Our materials scientists determined that if we increased the percentage of elements X and Y in our aluminum alloy, we could greatly improve its resistance to corrosion. But changing the blend of an alloy does not just affect its anti-corrosive qualities; it also changes the machinability, heat characteristics, and mechanical strength. The alloy we were using was an industry standard, and the result of many years of research and experience. There is no perfect material, and finding the best blend of alloy properties is extremely difficult.

Our materials team made a recommendation for an improved alloy and Dr Hu started working closely with a production engineer named Joey Lee at our supplier. Together, they dived into

After making more than 200 test pieces, we finally perfected both the formula of the alloy and the right balance of properties.

the foundry for experiments and tests. Outside in the Shenzhen summer it was tropical, and inside the foundry it often topped 50°C; it was like a sauna in there.

Dr Hu and Lee spent over three months in that environment, adjusting and testing their new alloys. It was a frustrating process. One adjustment might make the metal more corrosion-resistant, but its heat dissipation would suffer. They would correct the heat conduction issue, only to discover that now the strength of the metal was not up to standard. The perfect balance of qualities eluded them for three months, until they finally found a formula that was four times as resistant to corrosion. But the formability was not good: the alloy would not come out of the mold easily.

Dr Hu made a suggestion to change the proportions of two elements to improve mold performance, but his suggestion represented a significant break with standard alloy casting practice. Lee was very dubious, but he thought that he should give it a try, out of respect for Dr Hu. Remarkably, it worked. Formability was much improved and parts came easily out of their molds. Another few rounds of tweaking, and the formula was close to perfect. For Lee, it was an extremely exciting breakthrough.

It took another 11 months of testing to prove that the new alloy would stand up to the stresses of the many different uses that Huawei required. After making more than 200 test pieces, we finally perfected both the formula of the alloy and the right balance of properties. Our final material was four times more corrosion-resistant; heat dissipation was improved by 30%; and formability was better. We had truly invented a new class of aluminum alloy.

Want a Beautiful Antenna? Slim It Down, Give It a Facelift

In 2012, we set targets for reducing the physical size and weight of our active antenna units. The weight of the radome – the protective outer hood of the antenna – should be cut by one third and the thickness of the antenna should also be reduced by one third. We set up two teams to work on the two targets. Dr Zhang led the weight-reduction team and Stefan Feuchtinger from our Germany research centre led the size-reduction team.

Slimming away one third of the thickness of an antenna is no small operation. It's not so much a facelift as a complete facial reconstruction. Feuchtinger drank a lot of coffee in his initial brainstorming period, as he tried to come up with a feasible approach. During one meeting, he asked his team: "Why are TVs getting thinner and thinner?" Everyone knew the answer to that: cathode ray tubes had been replaced by LCD screens. That made them realize that a structural rearrangement wasn't going to be enough to achieve their one-third reduction. They would need new technology.

Now that they had the beginnings of an idea, Feuchtinger's team listed all the factors that make the biggest impact on the thickness of an antenna and came up with a novel idea. They wanted to reduce the cross-section of the radiating element by one third, but this was something that had never been attempted before, so there were no past best practices to look at. They had to figure out every step of the way for themselves.

They built an initial prototype, but when they tested it, the results were very poor. Feuchtinger and his team did not give up. They were sure that the idea they had was correct, so they started over again, building their simulation and their real prototype bit by bit. After five months of careful comparison and analysis, they finally found the cause of the issue.

The radome is an antenna's suit of armour. It protects the antenna from gale-force winds, torrential rain, baking sun, and freezing temperatures. But it must leave radio signals unimpeded, and ensure good electromagnetic performance. Radomes are usually made of fibreglass, which is strong and has the required electromagnetic properties. But it is heavy. We needed to find a material that had the strength and electrical properties of fibre-glass, but was significantly lighter.

Li Jiaren was our technical lead for macromolecular materials. He first compared all known plastics against our specific requirements, but he quickly found that there was no material that we could use directly to make a lighter radome. So Li went to visit some of the major research facilities and fabricators of macromolecular materials, both in and outside China. After a few initial discussions, he and his research partners settled on one particular raw material, which they thought they could adapt to make the hoods that we wanted. There were a lot of technical problems to be resolved first, however.

Huawei's research arm, 2012 Labs, decided to launch a collaborative project. We would work with external partners to develop the materials and the manufacturing processes needed for light radomes. After an agreement was reached, Li quickly got to work with his collaborators. In the materials lab, they carried out many studies of material properties and machining processes. Using one raw material as a base, they altered the formula and additives in the manufacturing process, and improved its properties and workability, testing and refining as they went. It was a process like making dough: you need just the right blend of flour, yeast, water, oil, and salt to create the perfect loaf of bread.

After a year and a half's effort, the material required for light radomes was finally ready, but forming it into the correct shape was another challenge.

The first molding processes did not go well, and it took two weeks before they were able to make the first completed prototype. When they handed the prototype to Dr Zhang, he put the semi-spherical cover on the floor and stamped on it. The radome flattened under his foot, but as he raised his leg, it popped back into shape, completely undamaged. Everyone was very excited to see this success. The testing department took the prototype for a full battery of specialized tests and found that there was still a problem during low-temperature impact tests.

Dr Zhang and Li went to visit the manufacturer to see if they could resolve the issue. One of the plastics specialists there told them that they were having a lot of problems. The radomes were coming out with uneven surfaces, weld lines, and voids. Dr Zhang and Li started looking for the problem. They tried cooling, annealing, and adjusting the mold. Then they stood and watched as the plastic poured, and hoped that the result would be a perfect product.

What came out looked very good: the surface was smooth, and the size was correct. It looked like the light radome that everyone had been hoping for. After a week of practice, the supplier was able to consistently produce high-quality radomes, and the performance of the new series in the low-temperature impact tests was significantly better. Our radomes now met all the required standards and could be put into use.

They say nothing is impossible for those with enough determination. Huawei's active antenna units keep on getting smaller and lighter, and our customers are happy with the results. They are now in use all over the world, and in 2015 alone we shipped over 100,000 units.

Easy Macro, an antenna light enough for one person to lift

We're Going to Be Around for a Long Time

You have to face extinction to truly know what it means to survive. The reason we were able to survive is that we focused on our customers' needs, innovated, delivered high-quality products and solutions, and created value for our customers.

2011: Huawei proposes the Single Antenna idea, a multi-band antenna for today's complex networks.

2012: Launches the comprehensive Single Antenna solution and the industry's first beamforming active antenna unit.

2013: Launches the EasyRET solution and SBS antenna architecture, placing us at the forefront of the antenna industry.

2013: Produces the industry's first five-band antenna, including the 800/900 MHz band, without any increase in size, resolving the antenna problem posed by LTE.

2013: Launches the FA/D 3D remote electrical tilt antenna, resolving a key problem for TD-LTE networks.

2014: Launches the world's first ultra-broadband multi-beam antenna, prompting widespread adoption of 6-sector technology.

2015: Launches G/D/P platforms and AAU3961, resolving a key problem for 4.5G networks.

2015: Huawei antennas become the industry's top seller: over 100,000 AAUs shipped.

2016: Launches the industry's first 9-sector multi-beam antenna and six-band 4.5G antenna.

2016: Conducts the first Massive MIMO field tests, launching 5G antenna technology.

2014–2016: Wins four consecutive Global Telecoms Business awards for our innovations in antennas.

Over the last six years, the Antenna Business Unit has lived up to the expectations of the company, and has survived and thrived. Looking forward, we plan to be around for a long, long time.

The Fourth Global Antenna & AAU Summit in Rome

Celebration in mid-2015 of the Antenna Business Unit's R&D successes

Seizing the Strategic High Ground

By Dai Xizeng

'Sages' of the Industry

I left China for my first-ever overseas standards conference in October 2008. The conference was held at Agilent's Edinburgh plant. Everything was new and strange to me. The setup was very much like a training classroom and it was packed full of more non-Chinese people than I'd ever seen in one room before. Sitting at the front was the chair of the conference and a secretary, and everyone who wanted to speak raised their hand and patiently waited for the one microphone to be handed around.

After a little while I realized that, though there were nearly 100 people present, only a very small number of people were actually speaking. There were contingents of a dozen or so people from both of the other two big equipment vendors, and they spoke with utter authority. They had sharp insights, fully worked-out ideas and, whenever a key question was brought up, they would announce, "We are conducting a detailed study on that right now, and we'll pass on the results as soon as we have them."

There was one other person at the conference who attracted my attention. He was the only representative from his company at the conference, but he had comments on every topic. He had a head of white hair and sharp eyes hidden behind his glasses. He spoke softly and slowly. During the breaks I saw him sitting alone, and people from other companies would periodically come up and talk to him. I saw that when he was in conversation, he seemed in no rush to express his own view, nor did he ask a lot of questions. But, when he did ask a question, it often seemed to reset the entire conversation. For me, attending my first ever big conference, he seemed like some sort of sage of the industry.

I realized that this was what a standards organization was like: a group of people with mature, well-defined rules and processes; a group who knew how to present proposals, debate, compromise, and arrive at consensus, all according to pre-agreed processes. That was how they advanced wireless communications technology, step by step.

Inside the conference hall

The First Steps Are the Hardest

Huawei had just joined this mature community and was running into some problems. We were struggling to fit in. First of all, there was the language barrier. At that point, most of us on the standards team had been educated in Chinese universities. We hadn't studied abroad and, though we'd taken English classes for 20 years or more, we still didn't have great reading or writing skills. Engaging and debating in English required a massive effort. Representatives from other companies came from all over the world and spoke English with a bewildering variety of accents. They used different terminologies, their grammar wasn't always standard, and it took a while before I was able to train my ear. At first it took all my concentration to just make out the words they were saying.

We needed real new technologies and ideas if we were to start scoring some hits in the ever-so-civilized battle of global standards.

There were also gaps in our knowledge of the technology. I remember one meeting when I was talking to a representative from another company. He started by saying, "This proposal of yours is the best one you have produced so far." I thought he was actually praising our proposal but, without pause, he immediately launched into a detailed critique. There are problems here, there are problems there ... by the time he'd finished, I realized he was actually saying the proposal was not much good. His initial praise had been nothing but a polite opener. At the time, I was very upset, but looking back now, I can see that he was right. We were not yet up to speed with our grasp of the technical issues.

But, neither of these were the core problem. What frustrated and hurt us most in those early years was that we were ignored. Often it felt like we didn't even exist. Whenever the representatives from other companies read their proposals, or made a point, everyone would listen carefully and engage in heated discussion. But when our proposals were read out, we were met with silence. No one responded or asked us any questions. During the coffee breaks, our peers from other companies would gather in knots of two or three for lively debate over some issue or other. But we were just wallflowers, seemingly stuck in a parallel universe to everyone else. If you haven't experienced it, it's hard to imagine how painful it is to be shut out like that. All your confidence is sapped out of you. How were we going to make our voice heard?

We knew that we couldn't allow the situation to continue. Huawei was determined to become a technology leader and a global player. To do that, Huawei needed a presence inside the standards organizations, and the standards team was on the cutting edge of that process. We had to find a way to get on the inside, to integrate into the standards bodies. And there were no shortcuts. We were just going to have to study up and smarten up. Study up meant that we needed to do better on the technical side. We needed real new technologies and ideas if we were to start scoring some hits in the ever-so-civilized battle of global standards. Smarten up meant learning to sell our ideas. Sometimes having good technology is not enough. It has to be an idea that you can market within the standards bodies and to the whole industry.

Saying Goodbye to 'Good Enough'

To help get us up and running on the technical side, in 2008 Huawei began to increase investment in learning the 3GPP standards (3rd Generation Partnership Project, the international standards body for wireless communications). We hired a number of people with lengthy experience in R&D and standards. Working with these old hands was a revelation for us novices. It wasn't just the level of technical knowledge they had; it was the way they went about their work: focused, rigorous, exacting.

They say the best workmen spend as much time sharpening their tools as they do carrying out their work. The first step to learning better technical skills was building a big enough simulator. If you want to build a plane, you need a wind tunnel. If you want to study nuclear physics, you need a particle accelerator. And, if you want to design wireless networks, you need a fully functional simulator. Once you've got it, then you can really start empirically quantifying how good your new technologies are.

This was an eye-opening idea for us. When we were starting out, we spent our time just reading about all the different protocols. It had never even crossed our minds to make the huge investment of time and money required to build a new simulator. In any case, given the level of expertise that we had, we were far from certain that we would succeed in building it.

The whole department got together in one small meeting room in our Beijing office. A technical leader stood at the whiteboard sketching out a long, twisted process diagram.

Then he stood back, pointed at it and said, "We have two months to make this." All of us let out one big gasp. From where we were standing, rank beginners in the field, it just seemed absurd. But, starting that day, led by our experienced experts, our young crew began a radical overhaul of our old, creaking simulator.

We had inspiring team slogans. We had Everest-style ambitions. But the realities of the day-to-day work were hard and dull. To build a simulator, the main thing you have to do is lots and lots of V&V – verification and validation testing. We had pages and pages of dense formulas and parameter tables, and our job was to vary each parameter from 0.1 to 0.95, in increments of 0.1, and test the performance of the decoder at every value. There were several different types of modulation to be tested, so in total we had to simulate 850 different curves. And every curve had a few dozen different signal-to-noise ratios to be tested. Every day, we sat around the servers, watching dozens of processes running in parallel, ready to jump in when a problem arose.

Dr Dai Xizeng, vice chair of 3GPP RAN4

When we had finally got our simulator up and running, it immediately revealed a number of problems in the technologies we had. That was quite a shock. If we had continued without a proper step-by-step process of verification and validation, and presented these faulty technologies at standards conferences, then we could have caused quite some damage to Huawei's reputation. They would have looked down on us. It made us all realize the importance of rigour in our work.

It took many sleepless nights, and many long, tiresome days. But, finally, we got the underlying processes for our simulator to work properly. We now had the system we needed to properly assess the quality of our own technologies. At future standards conferences, we too would be able to stand up and announce with full confidence: "We ran a full simulation, and under conditions X, Y, and Z, solution A outperformed solution B by precisely this much." From that point on, the proposals we submitted had more substance behind them, and they started to attract more serious attention.

Technology Matters Most

The completion of the simulator was just the start of the real work, of course. If we were going to start making a name for ourselves, we needed to produce some real technological innovations.

I remember a standards conference held in Athens a few years ago. A Huawei executive who came with us said, "Huawei has plenty of competitive products and we have a good market share. What we are missing is new technologies that everyone knows belong to Huawei."

We were ramping up investment in our global research capacity in wireless technologies at the time. Beijing, Shanghai, Kista (a 'science city' in Sweden built around one of the campuses of the KTH Royal Institute of Technology), Texas, Ottawa – we set up research teams all over the world. We had been working on wireless technologies for many years, and now we had experienced people, the background, and a growing team. The conditions were ripe for R&D to produce a series of heavyweight new products.

In 2010, Huawei created a landmark new technology: the multimode base station. With just a software upgrade, we enabled customers to switch easily between 2G, 3G, and 4G, so that mobile phone users all over the globe could gain equal access to the same networks. This technology gained industry-wide support as soon as it was released.

In September 2013, at an International Telecommunication Union (ITU) Asia-Pacific meeting, Huawei made the first proposal to integrate unlicensed spectrum (i.e., spectrum that is free to use everywhere in the world). For telecom operators, it offered a free source of new spectrum; for users, it promised faster connections, anytime, anywhere.

Also in 2013, Huawei started applying wireless technologies in the new area of the internet of things. We pushed the idea of using a narrowband air interface that offered good breadth of coverage at low cost. It could be used for remote reading of electricity meters and in telemedicine.

Although 4G technology had been available for some time by then, 5G was still several years in the future. How could we show the public that communications technology was still evolving and improving? From 2012 onwards, Huawei had been thinking about how to extend and evolve 4G technology. We wanted to give the industry a new generation of technology that they could reference as they planned, produced, marketed, and serviced their wireless communications products. And subscribers would benefit from the higher quality of telecom services.

After a period of development and discussion, we finally decided to name our new generation of technologies 4.5G. Within the industry, we used the name agreed with our peers: LTE-Advanced Pro. At the 3GPP conference in Mexico in April 2016, I was given a T-shirt with the LTE-Advanced Pro logo, the technology which Huawei had proposed as 4.5G. I felt incredibly proud as I put it on. The creation of the new 4.5G generation of technologies was a historic turning point. For the first time, Huawei had taken the lead in defining a new standard.

This series of Huawei-branded new technologies brought us the victories we needed on the standards battlefield.

Seizing the Strategic High Ground

Our technological successes gave the standards team more and more confidence. We were on the front lines of the standards battle and the objective of the standards team had never changed: we wanted our technology written into international standards and shared with the whole industry. So, our representatives in the standards organizations devoted themselves to winning this battle of intellectual properties. You have to love the fight to win the fight, and we were now able to stand on the shoulders of some seriously impressive technologies and products. We learned as we went, accumulated experience, and grew from young upstarts into practised operators.

The first time we were able to score a decisive victory over a senior representative from a major competitor was at the 3GPP meeting in Taipei in 2011. The topic of the meeting was a point on which we had been stuck for six months, and this meeting was to be the final decision. We obtained all the supporting information we could from the product teams. We produced strong, credible analyses, and we made sure we had the support of many equipment manufacturers. On the last day of the meeting, we engaged our counterpart from the competing company in fierce debate. Finally, the chair asked whether there were any other oppositions to our proposal. The last doubter changed their vote to neutral and, finally, our competitor had to concede the point to us. This meeting was not only a technical victory; it gave us enormous confidence as well.

After this meeting, the big telecom operators started to recognize our technical skills and agreed to work more with us in the future. In the elevator after the meeting, a representative from another company said to me, "You are getting better and better."

I chaired my first ever breakout session in Dresden, Germany, in February 2012. The chair of the working group later told me he was very pleased with how the session went.

In June 2014, I attended my first ever 3GPP plenary at Sophia Antipolis, Europe's largest high-tech zone, located in southern France. At this meeting I was able to get a new work item accepted for the first time. Then in August 2015, in Beijing, I was honoured to be appointed deputy chair of a working group.

Just a few years ago, there were no standards organization officials from Huawei. Now we have 90 experienced standards representatives[1] who serve as chairs, deputy chairs, or similar in international standards bodies including the ITU, Institute of Electrical and Electronics Engineers (IEEE), and 3GPP, where they work on standards for GSM, UMTS, LTE, 5G, and future evolutions. We are playing a direct role in setting the world's standards.

The Huawei team in the RAN4 Working Group

The Huawei team in the RAN1 Working Group

For the 2G standards, we were just an observer. In 3G, we were a follower. By 4G/4.5G, we were an active participant and leader. This progress came about because we maintained our focus and committed to investing the necessary time and funds.

Now the 5G era has begun. The Huawei teams are throwing themselves into the grand new project of 5G with more confidence and enthusiasm than ever. Huawei is now a key player in global standards. We are sure that we have even more contributions to make.

Note

A standards representative is a person who represents their company at an international standards organization. They submit technical proposals, participate in debates and ultimately decide the final form of technical communications standards. Reps convey the views of their company on technology and industry issues, engage with subject specialists, and once consensus is reached, develop protocols and specifications to be used by the whole industry. Their work is fundamental to the development of the communications sector.

What Goes into a Blockbuster Phone?

By Merlin Zhou

For more than ten years, a particular memory from my time in India has stuck with me. I was at a roadside shop in a remote mountain village. The villagers were all lined up, each holding a SIM card in their hand. They were anxiously waiting to use the only mobile phone in the village. Dozens of villagers took turns inserting their own SIM card into the phone, and made calls to friends and relatives in Mumbai or New Delhi. Each of them had a happy grin on their face. The phone had no brand logo, but I could tell that it was one of Huawei's. This memory has always brought me joy over the years, because I know that in an inconspicuous corner of the world, a Huawei phone connected a group of people to their loved ones.

The Huawei Mate 7 smartphone was launched in September 2014. A colleague from the sales team pointed at photographs of seas of people buying Huawei phones at our flagship stores: "This is the scene in Shanghai. This is the scene in Beijing." All in an instant, that sense of happiness and satisfaction that I felt all those years ago in India came back to me – Huawei phones have reached almost every corner of the world. They are connecting tens of millions of consumers and are indispensable in their daily lives.

However, every one of the Mate 7's popular features – the large screen, the all-metal body, fingerprint recognition and its user interface – was developed through a process fraught with errors and mistakes. In fact, it was that process of trial and error that enabled us to find the correct approach.

How Big Is a Big Screen?

Let's talk about the screen. The Huawei Mate and Mate 2 both had large screens, but the body of the phone was too big. Customers complained: "It seems like Huawei thinks size is everything. It's too thick and too heavy. It's almost impossible to hold!"

Of course, we want every handset to be a bestseller, so these criticisms were a slap in the face for me. Once bitten, twice shy, so when we started work on the Mate 7 in 2013, we started by thinking from the customer's perspective. What was the largest acceptable size of screen? Could anything be subtracted in terms of thickness and weight?

We tried many sizes, from 5.7 inches to 7 inches. After we had made a series of prototypes, we invited a consumer focus group to come and try out how the handsets felt. We picked a group that included men and women of various ages and heights. We found that the 6-inch screen was the absolute limit for most people. Any larger than that and the handset became difficult to control. It lost its convenience and ease of use. We also slimmed down the thickness of the handset, reducing it from the 9 mm of the Mate 2 to less than 8 mm. At the time, this made the Mate 7 the thinnest of all smartphones in the same class of screen size.

Another thing that made customers unhappy with previous handsets was the large black border around the screen. If the handset body was of a relatively light colour, then the black border surrounding the screen would clash with the body, which didn't look attractive. So, one small goal we set for the Mate 7 was to minimize the black border.

This necessitated developing a new technology – narrow bezel adhesive. Just like squeezing toothpaste from a tube, the adhesive is applied around the edges of the handset shell, and then the screen is fixed into place. The narrower the adhesive surface, the smaller the body of the handset can be.

It doesn't sound all that technical, but the difficulty comes when you are trying to mass-produce the product. At first, we applied the adhesive by hand, but this was not precise enough. Later, we introduced robotic arms to handle the task, but they turned out to be less than cooperative. The adhesive had to be applied to a surface less than 1 mm wide. It was like trying to write a message on a strand of hair. Our robotic arms would drift either left or right. Sometimes they would get several dozen in a row perfect, but then drift again. It was infuriating.

It would take days to make each adjustment. The factory staff would exclaim in exasperation, "It's just a fraction of a millimeter.

You can't even see the difference! Why make such a fuss about it?" I would be lying if I said I didn't feel sorry to see one box after another of discarded components. But we pushed through to get it done right. Even though it seemed like a small issue, we had a responsibility to our customers.

In order to improve the precision of the process, we installed cameras on the robotic arms. This way the machine could 'see' exactly where the handset shell was positioned, which allowed the adhesive to be placed in the right location. But this was still not enough.

Using the right type of adhesive was also critical. If it was too viscous, the screen wouldn't adhere. If it was too dilute, the joint wouldn't hold. You had to give it sufficient time to dry, but leaving it too long slowed down the whole production line. From among the countless varieties of adhesive, we selected a dozen or so and conducted many rounds of testing. We looked at whether the glued joints remained reliable in high and low temperatures, and under impacts. Finally we found the best possible blend.

Richard Yu, CEO of Huawei's Consumer Business Group,
shows off the large screen during the Mate 7 release

We also developed a clamp to anchor the screen more tightly as the glue dried. The setting time was reduced from eight hours down to two, and we achieved a thinner border than ever before. The final phone really was just four edges, four corners, and a screen, which meant that the big screen didn't translate into an awkwardly large body.

Partnership with an Automobile Manufacturer

Prior to the Mate 7, the majority of handsets on the market had plastic bodies. There was no real tactile quality, and consumers were weary of that design. Would it be possible to make a metal body? Anyone involved in handset manufacture knows that metal processing is not easy, and you get a lot of defects.

We'd had some bad experiences trying to work with metal before. In 2012, we made our first metal body for the D2 smartphone. It was a classic case of 'fools rush in': we made the decision to use stainless steel because it is hard and strong, and we used a standard computer numerical control tool to cut the parts. The result was that only 20% of our parts met quality standards. If it wasn't a problem with size, then it was scratches and other aesthetic defects. We couldn't even produce 1,000 units per day, resulting in ultra-long production runs and exorbitant costs.

When working on the Mate 7, we began to look around at what others were doing in the industry to find different processing techniques. We carefully sifted through all possible suppliers in the manufacturing industry and our attention was drawn to an automobile manufacturer. Even though they were producing cars, they had in-depth experience in metal processing. We wondered if they could also produce handsets.

This was a bold move that no one had tried before. The supplier used stamping technology, which used heavy equipment to stamp out vehicle bodies. The machine would pound the metal pieces into the desired shape for our handsets. With this type of pre-forming, we were able to cut costs and shorten our production time. This equipment was more than 3m in height, and 4–5m wide, weighing 110 tons. Using it to stamp out handset bodies was like Godzilla crushing an ant. It seemed a bit overboard, but it did get the job done. Every time it thumped down, the bang of the press was deep and resonating, a truly impressive thing to witness.

At the start, we were not able to control the power of the machine effectively, and a large number of handset shells twisted after they came out of the stamp. We were not getting the precision that we needed. So, we decided to add two annealing processes for better precision. This involved placing the shells in a kiln at 120°C for two hours. However, more steps in the process meant a longer production time.

To speed things up, the R&D team came out to the factory and started experimenting. They took samples from the kilns wearing special protective gloves. Each time they entered the kiln it was like a high-temperature sauna and they had to do this several times each day. As time went on, I noticed that a number of overweight team members were slimming down considerably. Some of our colleagues back at the labs joked that it was like a hot yoga class: "Seems to be working wonders for your figure!"

Mobile phones require a much higher degree of precision than automobile parts. In vehicle bodies, a gap of several millimeters is acceptable, whereas a gap of less than a millimeter in a mobile phone makes for an obvious quality issue. The supplier worked closely with us to make all the process improvements we could think up. More than 20 technicians from the supplier would squeeze into the workshop with us each day to review each step: stamping, molding, grinding, and polishing. How much pressure should be used in the press? What temperature and what duration were best for the annealing? We relentlessly tweaked each parameter, and in the process we built up a strong relationship with the supplier.

Finally, our stamped shells were consistently passing quality assurance checks. That was the ultimate award for our efforts over more than 180 busy days and nights.

Secrets of the One-Second Unlock

One of the surprises the Mate 7 delivered to customers was the phone's fingerprint scanner. Many people originally dismissed the fingerprint lock, but later it came to be their favourite feature. With the screen off, and without pressing any buttons, the handset owner can place a finger on the sensor area on the back of the phone and the screen will unlock in less than one second. Fingerprint recognition can also be used when making mobile payments.

However, many people were surprised to see that the fingerprint scanner is on the back of the phone. In fact, there were also heated discussions within Huawei about this. Some people thought it should be placed on the front, since this was the industry standard. A number of other phone makers had tried to place the scanner on the back, all unsuccessfully. But, after careful consideration, we decided that if we were to add a fingerprint scanner on the front of a 6-inch handset, it would have too much of an impact on size and appearance. Another consideration was that placing your thumb on a front button is awkward, and you have to hold the phone out to one side. This is why we ultimately decided to keep the scanner on the back. In the end, our decision was vindicated: Mate 7 users gave us very positive feedback about that part of the design.

So, we knew what we wanted to do, but how could we turn the design into reality? We had to find an outstanding manufacturer. Back in 2012, we began to track the progress of manufacturers of fingerprint scanners. One of our research centres set us up on a 'date' with a company that developed fingerprint scanners. After a short period of discussion, both sides thought a collaboration was very feasible, but the details still had to be ironed out.

The fingerprint scanners manufactured by this company were mostly used on common combination locks. To place the component on a handset would require making a complete scanner module prior to installation, which was easy enough. What had us worried was the difference between a phone lock and a combination lock for a door or safe. Combination locks are generally used only a few times a day, whereas customers might lock and unlock their phones hundreds of times a day. This presented a significant challenge in terms of the lifespan of the fingerprint scanner and the speed of the scan.

The depth of the sensor area was also the subject of dozens of back-and-forth experiments. This was an issue that would directly impact user experience, and it was a technical issue affecting the speed of fingerprint recognition. We didn't know what to do, so we just worked it out from first principles. We made several dozen models of the scanner, each one with the metal outer rim a different thickness and diameter. Then we brushed ink on the sensor area. We pressed our fingers onto the sensor, then pressed them on a piece of blank paper, and compared the clarity and size of each fingerprint. That was how we tested the shape of the sensor area for our scanner.

After a process of adjustment, the fingerprint scan time was cut from 1,300 milliseconds down to 1,000 milliseconds. This meant that we could get the phone unlocked in less than one second: a true 'one-touch' unlock.

'Black Box' Security

So, we had achieved agility and accuracy, but all the scanner did was convert a fingerprint into an image. The question of security was still to be resolved. We had to have a perfect answer for our customers.

We spoke to many different R&D departments to find a solution to the security issue, including our chip specialists. After many rounds of talks and head-to-head comparisons between different proposals, we came up with a unique idea: would it be possible to place the secure fingerprint scanning system on a separate segment of the chip? It would be a totally opaque 'black box'. After you stored something on it, you could not touch or remove that information. All that part of the chip would do is answer 'yes' or 'no' based on a fingerprint scan.

They say you
should 'eat your
own dog food'.

To achieve this, we developed an independent 'Secure OS' for the chip's secure 'Trust Zone'. All the encryption and decryption processes for fingerprints were moved wholesale out of the external Android system and into the Secure OS. To this day, the Mate 7 fingerprint scan solution is recognized as one of the most secure systems in the world.

The fingerprint scanner was one of the highlights of the Mate 7 for users

They say you should 'eat your own dog food'. This means that a company should be willing to use its own products for internal operations. In this case, that meant using our own phones. In order to expose any potential issues, we used the prototype handsets ourselves for a period of time. We uncovered a variety of situations in which the phone could be activated unintentionally. To solve this issue, the fingerprint scanner was indented further into the body, and software algorithms helped prevent accidental unlocking.

Fan Idea Turns to Gold

For many users, a more obvious change was in the software system. Previously, when you turned on a Huawei phone, the background and icons were a rainbow of different colours and designs. We had received a lot of complaints about this. "It's hideous!" many people said. This time around, the entire theme was an elegant combination of points, lines, and circles – including the icons for the message app, gallery, and clock. It was simpler and much more attractive.

But being aesthetically pleasing is not enough. The usability of the apps also directly impacts user experience. Here I have to mention a brilliant idea that we got from a Huawei fan – we call them 'Huafans'. In early 2014, we held a Huafan meet-and-greet in Shanghai. One fan asked a question that stumped everyone present: "Why is it not possible to switch quickly between the dialler, contacts, and message apps?" Our product manager for the contacts app thought for a moment, then said almost to himself, "Right! If we could swipe left or right in the contacts menu to make a call or send a text message without having to open a different app, it would be much more convenient!"

At that time, we were just developing the latest version of Huawei's EMUI operating system for phones. All our colleagues were racking their brains trying to think up new functions. When they heard this idea, they were stunned that they hadn't thought of it themselves and quickly got down to developing the function.

The biggest hurdles were in the time it took to load up an app. It previously only took 500 milliseconds to open your phone contacts, a literal blink of an eye. But, after the three apps were combined, load time was really slow. It took more than three seconds to open. You would stare at the loading hourglass turning around and around, but the page would take forever to load, and sometimes it would whitescreen out. We tried a number of different solutions, but we weren't getting anywhere.

Hands-on tryouts of the new phone at Huawei before the official release

At that point, one of our software architects, Liang Yuning, took the initiative: "Let me give it a shot!" He read up on the latest approaches to database loading and process scheduling, and came upon the approach of phased opening. Users don't need to use multiple functions simultaneously, so, if the user opens the contacts app, that function should load first. The other two apps (the dialler and message apps) could be loaded quietly in the background. This way the wait time could be reduced to less than 700 milliseconds. As opening the app always triggered a little loading animation anyway, at this speed the user wouldn't perceive any problem.

After completing this new function, we invited a few dozen Huafans to give it a go. One user sighed in satisfaction: "It's like being in a restaurant and having the choice of three different cuisines, rather than having to change restaurants. It's great!" This response made us truly happy.

Hammer-Hardened Before Release

"Today my phone fell off my desk. It hit the ground with a smack and my heart broke! But the phone didn't break!" This was a relieved comment left online by a Huafan.

Before we release a product, we consider a wide variety of possibilities. At the Huawei Device Reliability Laboratory, each day there are more than 1,000 handsets turned on 24/7 for stability testing. All performance issues are noted down. We carry out drop tests on the six surfaces and four corners of the phone. Using laboratory equipment, we drop the phones from different heights. When a phone hits a marble slab, we hear a sharp smack, but the Mate 7 remains intact and undamaged. There is also a high-speed camera next to the equipment, which records the deformation as the handset hits the marble. This data is analysed to improve the overall product strength.

In addition to this, there are thousands of tumble tests, hundreds of twist tests, a test involving exposure to several dozen hours of solar radiation, a test involving hundreds of thousands of taps on the touchscreen, and a test involving hundreds of thousands of button presses. Only after rigorous testing are products given the green light for market release.

Looking back on my work on Huawei's mobile phones, I realize that I've been involved in the development of many different models. Not all of them were successful. In fact, many met with failure. Good phones don't just appear out of nowhere. It was precisely these setbacks, the mistakes we made, that allowed us to grow and ultimately end up with a smartphone loved by many, many people.

Trying out a new phone that you have personally helped to develop is like cuddling your own baby. You can never get enough of it. As an engineer, my greatest sense of achievement comes from seeing more and more people using Huawei phones and recommending them to their friends and family.

The Office at Your Fingertips

By Meteor Liu

Can you imagine a world in which you could use your mobile phone to punch in at work, check and send emails, or even claim expenses? Huawei AnyOffice Mobile Solution enables you to work on a variety of jobs via your mobile phone. Millions of users enjoy this app, and it helps many businesses quickly transform from work that is office-based and PC-reliant to an approach in which employees can work wherever and whenever they wish.

The idea for the design was hit upon by chance in 2010.

It All Started from a Scandal Involving Phone Hacking

At the end of 2010, Nokia still played a leading role in the mobile phone sector. Smart devices had just arrived on the scene. Back then, I was an engineering nerd who had been working at Huawei for three years. My job had nothing to do with mobile apps.

One day, I received a phone call from an overseas Huawei office: a scandal involving phone hacking had erupted in that country. The senior officials were desperate to find a secure telephone solution to avoid a recurrence of the incident they were experiencing. They respected Huawei's professionalism in cybersecurity and hoped that we could provide them with an end-to-end secure solution.

With great foresight, the manager of my product development team (PDT) at the time saw that mobile apps and mobile security products would soon be a major force in the industry. He convened all the members of the team for a brainstorming session. We delved deep into everything from technical solutions to product development plans and blueprints. At the end of the meeting, I could see that everyone was happy with the outcome. It seemed as though success was all but guaranteed.

From that point on, our team jumped right into the development of the mobile app. The mainstay mobile operating systems were Symbian and BlackBerry. Android and the iPhone iOS were new to the market. As we had no experience in developing apps for mobile devices, the process was a journey fraught with anxiety for the team. We spent a whole week building a development environment for the app, then it crashed the moment we installed it on the Android system. We had little know-how and no way to effectively troubleshoot issues. All we could do was check the source code of the system line by line. Our persistence and hard work paid off in the end. Forty days into our endeavour, we finally succeeded. We used a mobile phone to call another phone through wifi connection. When my teammate and I heard each other's voice over the line, we couldn't help but shout out in joy and excitement.

We continued our efforts for three months and came up with a first version for testing. We sent the version to the field, full of confidence and high hopes. Two days later, we received feedback saying that the voice over wifi was of poor quality and almost unrecognizable under certain circumstances, such as network switching. The feedback made my heart sink. There was nothing to do but go back to the drawing board, locate the faults, and resolve the issue. At first, I was only able to address one issue every few days. As my skills developed, I could address several issues each day.

Another four months went by and the app was nearing completion. By then, it stood up to testing and use in the field. Its communications quality lived up to expectations under normal and harsh conditions. The confidence of my teammates was infectious, enabling me to confidently deliver the finished product to the customer. The product eventually went live and senior officials began using our secure app for mobile calls. They could finally rest assured that their calls were secure and protected.

The Tortoise Wins the Race

The above case was only one success, however. Data traffic back then was expensive, and the conditions to allow for extensive use of secure phone apps weren't there yet. The experience we gained

Discussing issues with our mobile office applications with the customer

from the project in developing apps gave us what we needed to hit the ground running.

In early 2012, the smartphone business was booming. In view of the trends in the industry, Huawei decided to enable extensive mobile office applications, letting people work wherever and whenever needed. Thanks to our past experience in security and mobile app development, we were well positioned to take on this task. By seizing this opportunity, we hoped to build a mobile information platform for businesses.

Just after we finished the first version of our product, we got wind that one of our strategic customers was accepting bids for the development of such a product and was already testing versions provided by bidders. Two leading competitors already had dominance in this sector. If we won the bid, we would be able to roll out our products to a variety of sectors on a large scale. We immediately assigned our most capable go-getters to take our product to the customer.

Many of my teammates worked overnight in the office and even slept there so that they could continue working as soon as they woke up.

Who could have known that after so much work, what awaited us on the other side was a bucket of cold water over our heads? After talking with the customer, we learned that our competitors had already finished first-round testing and had earned their trust. We received information about the test cases provided by our competitors and found that our product lacked many of the functions of their solution. We had a very slim chance of winning. Despite this, we decided to set up a task force to be responsible for quickly enabling key functions in our product, and spent four days communicating with the customer.

The project was clearly very urgent. We wanted to get it done in one all-or-nothing attempt. Many of my teammates worked overnight in the office and even slept there so that they could continue working as soon as they woke up. We worked for four days straight and came up with a version for testing. Everything went well through the day as testing commenced. We were relieved. R&D staff even found some time in their busy schedule to return home for a well-deserved rest. However, at 8pm that evening, a critical issue was repeatedly detected in our version. Some teammates who had just left for the day and hadn't even arrived home yet were called back. We worked hard all night, but could not find the bug. We were anxious. The appointment with the customer to test our version was quickly approaching and we had no idea what to do next. We called colleagues who were on-site with the customer, asking them to do everything they could to win us one more day.

A tester then chimed in: "One of our previous versions did not have this issue. But we modified so many lines of code these past few days that it would be impossible to read through each line of code now." I was the configuration management operator of the task force. Upon hearing his words, I came up with an idea. The system automatically compiled a version each hour, so if we could figure out when exactly this issue started to occur, we could more easily troubleshoot the issue. Everyone agreed on this approach and got down to work verifying different versions. In this way, we eventually found the bug.

We continued to devote ourselves to the project and, by addressing several such issues, we gradually gained the upper hand and won the first application from the customer. Later, we went to the equipment rooms of the customer to help them launch the system across the country. When I saw the room full of equipment from our two competitors, tears came to my eyes. We had come a long way from our humble beginnings. I couldn't help but feel a sense of pride for our hard-earned success.

It was not until after the project had concluded that the customer told us candidly: "At the beginning of the testing, you knew nothing about the project. You were like a tortoise, lagging way behind in the race with your peers, who were as quick as hares. However, you were very responsive. The issues we detected were always addressed very quickly and the functionality we needed was all made available. Your product was totally transformed in the later stages of the project. A tortoise won the race. Well done."

How Could We Have Trouble With Such a Small User Base?

Towards the end of 2013, our app was being used by thousands of Huawei employees. The department tasked with running the app developed a half-year plan, hoping that mobile office functionality could be enabled for all of the hundreds of thousands of employees across the company. The intensive promotion quickly increased the user base of our app to 20,000.

But one evening in November of that year, the manager of the IT operating team called me, saying that the system had rebooted on its own. Worse still, after the reboot, some colleagues said that they could not log in to the system. We looked into the situation ourselves and were shocked to find we couldn't log in, either. Luckily, not many colleagues were accessing the system during these off-work hours. But if the login issue was not addressed before the start of work the following day, it would have a negative impact on business.

How could we address this urgent issue? I accessed the server remotely and found that the central processing unit (CPU) usage kept jumping to 100%, as it needed to process timeout alarms from user logins. After careful analysis, I found that the congestion was being caused by each user taking a prolonged amount of time to log in. The system just could not strike a balance, which meant no one could log in properly.

We needed to find a solution. I convened a task force right away. By 11pm that night, the system engineer suggested we should break the cycle by configuring the system to log in users in groups. If some of them could log in to the system, there wouldn't be so many people trying to log in simultaneously. With the exception of the login function, all other functions were multithreading. As long as users could successfully log in to the system, the system could stand the pressure. However, how could we control the automatic login of mobile users? The test manager came up with the idea of controlling the access scope of users via the system's firewall, thereby guiding the login of users in groups.

That was it. We started to implement the solution. Two hours later, all users were able to log in to the system and the CPU usage dropped back to normal. The PDT manager sent me home to take a break and asked me to come in early the next morning, as the system would see a surge of logins the next day. When I returned, I was happy to see that the operating pressure of the system was increasing only gradually, as we had expected. The system survived the first surge of logins.

The colleague who reported the issue mentioned that his team was even more anxious than us on the day that the issue had been detected. They were the ones who had put us in charge of this system so, if we received complaints, they would have to share a certain amount of the responsibility. Fortunately, we did not let them down. The operating team stopped promoting the app after the incident. However, the user base still expanded to 30,000 in four months. To meet the needs of a larger user base, we had to maintain the stability of the system, while optimizing the system architecture. We also drew lessons from internet companies on grey release, which helped us to metaphorically change each tyre on a bus travelling at high speed. In April 2014, the new version went live and was made available to all users. By June of the same year, the total number of users jumped to 80,000. The system was running stably, with fewer issues. We only needed to have a meeting with the operating team once a week, when just a few months prior we had been meeting them every day.

Today, this app is installed on more than 300,000 devices and used by over 200,000 internal users. All versions are verified on this system before official launch to the public. It's hard to imagine now those early days when it was so difficult to manage 20,000 users.

Presenting the AnyOffice app to our customers

Too Many Customer Requirements?

In 2013, the AnyOffice app was taking shape and we began delivering it to a customer. Before I brought it to them, I thought the app would address all of their stated requirements and that there wouldn't be any problems. Oh, how naive I was. The customer said the app required configuration before use, and this made it difficult to roll out. They asked us to address this issue immediately, otherwise they would return the product. I had trouble understanding this request when I heard it. Why couldn't this app be rolled out with a simple additional step for configuration? Nevertheless, our team looked into the issue and made it possible to use the app without any configuration being needed.

However, that wasn't the end of the story. After addressing the issue of accessibility, the customer made a new request. "The text in the mailing list is too small." Yes, sir. We can make it bigger. A few days later, the customer made another request: "Some users have said that the text is too large. It's tough on the eyes. Could you enable a function to allow adjustment of the font size?" I was a bit stunned when I heard this request. How could we satisfy each and every request from so many users? There was plenty of negative feedback from internal and external users: "The interface is not user-friendly"; "This prompt is terrible"; and "The font size is not consistent and the colours make me feel depressed." The complaints made me realize that, as a developer, we could not focus all our attention on the functional logic and parameter specifications when developing mobile apps. We had to think more about user experience.

I needed to change my mindset, so I tried to think of myself as a product manager in order to figure out how to develop a better product. How would I go about that? First of all, I immersed myself in the internet and became a connoisseur of mobile apps. Every night before I slept, I would find highlights of the latest top apps. I watched videos by internet gurus on how they improved user experience. I learned from product development masters about how they forged a keen sense of being able to detect anything wrong with a product. During this process, I honed my awareness of details and gained more experience. During the later stages of product development, we had a discussion that lasted until midnight, talking about where to place a button and how to restructure code to increase the response speed by just a single second. We also analysed competing products, surveyed users, and worked with experts from the user-centred design centre (UCD) to create a WeChat group for users to complain about our app. We also opened a real-time official account for public reviews. We started to use the DevOps model for crowd testing and established a UCD committee for collective review and decision-making.

Our app was significantly improved thanks to the collective wisdom we gained from these efforts. When we finally heard favourable comments from previously dissatisfied customers, we felt a sense of accomplishment for making a high-performance product.

Could You Do It Faster?

In May 2014, through half a year of determined effort, we achieved the strategic goal of decoupling AnyOffice from Any-Mail. With two separate clients, we could more flexibly deliver functionality related to the Bring Your Own Device (BYOD) solution – a trend in which companies allow staff to bring personally owned mobile devices to the workplace.

At that time, one of our customers, a bank, asked us to deliver the solution online. We assigned R&D experts to the customer's site to discuss the launch of the solution. The R&D experts spent a whole month communicating with the bank and commissioning on site. Soon after launch, the customer issued many new requirements aimed at making the app easier to use. Our reply was that, according to the company's product development process, we would need three months to meet the new requirements. The customer threw a string of rhetorical questions at the R&D representative in reply: "Is your company Huawei or not? Where is your customer-centric spirit? You need three months to enable such simple functionality?" The customer then continued: "We can find a firm that could do it in a couple of days. When we developed our own apps, we could deliver a version for testing every other day and a new official version each week. You have to do it faster!" We persuaded the customer to give us two weeks to deliver the new version and enable new functionality in an iterative manner.

Then, our R&D experts joined forces with experts from other domains to discuss how to better address customer requirements and ensure agile delivery. They even urged the company to start a project for piloting agile product development. This more agile model helped the project team to rank requirements and make quick decisions. The new model also enabled us to deliver functions and iterate new versions on a monthly basis.

To keep up with the fast pace of version releases, we gradually replaced manual testing with automated testing. Afterwards, automated testing was applied to all new requirements and the entire laboratory validation process was automated using scripts. The product would then be immediately published to the crowd-testing platform prior to large-scale application. It was also tested on a variety of devices to ensure compatibility. This ensured there was prompt feedback and a quick closed loop in product management. Allowing device users to directly participate in the evaluation of the product experience and quality also made them more aware of the ongoing improvements being made to AnyOffice. Eventually, we delivered a high quality solution on schedule. The fast and iterative delivery became a highly potent tool for us to win more customers.

Today, we are implementing strategic development and are aiming to create a full series of secure solutions for mobile information platforms geared towards businesses. The solutions cover end-to-end security, from data security of mobile devices, to cyber-security through firewalls at access points of business, and big data security. These efforts will continue to boost our competitiveness. I am now an R&D manager coordinating the work of R&D teams in Hangzhou (China), Beijing (China), Finland, and Canada. This post is a challenge for me, but I embrace it with confidence and courage.

I am lucky to have witnessed the leapfrog development of AnyOffice over the past six years. Many people use this app each day, enjoying the convenience brought about by having an office at their fingertips. Nothing in the world has made me more proud than seeing this become a reality.

Transmission at the Speed of Light

By Jeffrey Gao

"Lucent is the industry leader. How does the equipment you are making measure up to theirs?"

That was the question that our founder and CEO, Ren Zheng-fei, put to us one evening in 1998, when he dropped in unannounced at our lab. Since then, 18 years have flashed by and today we have a definitive answer to this question.

Green Team, World-Class Ambitions

1997 was a good year for China. The whole country was celebrating the return of Hong Kong to Chinese sovereignty. It also turned out to be a lucky year for me. In Shenzhen, just across the bay from Hong Kong, I was starting my career at Huawei.

Back then, I was working in the transmission network department, in charge of developing network devices that could handle data rates of up to 2.5G, using the synchronous digital hierarchy (SDH) protocol. We encountered many, many difficulties, and at one point we ran into a problem that we just could not solve, no matter what we tried. We had no choice but to call a vendor outside of China to ask for more information. None of us could speak English fluently, but it fell to me to make the phone call. I had to bite the bullet. I rehearsed in my head over and over again what I was going to say, but when I heard the voice on the other end of the line say, "Hello?" my mind went completely blank and I forgot every line I had prepared. "Please give us a demo board," I stammered. When the call was finally over, my teammates all yelled at me for not saying clearly what issue we were having. But unexpectedly, the vendor faxed the diagram of the demo board to us the very next day. That diagram helped us work through the issue. That was a very happy moment for me.

One year after we developed this product, I was sent to a small town in Chongqing to help set up some equipment for our customer there. Unexpectedly, I received a call from one of the company secretaries. She told me to get back to Shenzhen as fast as possible and start packing for a telecoms expo in Moscow.

In the chill of early spring, I flew to Moscow. Huawei was the only exhibitor from China at the event. Later, we won a contract to provide a set of SDH transmission equipment in Bryansk, and that got our whole international development off to a good start.

Next, we started to develop a range of multi-functional products with 10G of bandwidth. At the time, this speed was known as a tough target. Only the world's top companies had the capacity to create products at this level. But because I had worked on the 2.5G products, I was appointed product manager, leading a team of green young men as we took on this world-class challenge.

Looking back, it's obvious that we were 'fools rushing in'. We had no experience developing this type of equipment and there were no books or papers that we could use as a reference. So, we had to figure it all out ourselves. Every step of the way, we cast around for the right way to go next. We would try a number of different ideas, and test them to see if they worked.

We had many arguments over what kind of design we should use, and they often got quite heated. On one occasion, the staff in the lab next door thought there was a fist fight and hurried around to break it up. Sometimes the arguments would get more intense without any sign of agreement and, in the end, I had to step in and make a decision: we're going to do this, because I'm the boss.

But, despite all the differences of opinion, we were a tight-knit team. When we got off work, we would go to a small restaurant nearby, order a big plate of fried noodles and some shish kebabs, then chat and laugh the evening away. We were always direct with each other, saying exactly what we thought. That way, all the different possibilities and risks could be worked out. It was a good way to minimize the chances of making a big mistake.

Before we launched the product, we invited some of China's leading specialists in this technology to come to our manufacturing facility and run some tests. During this period, none of us went home at all. We laid down mats on the floor of our Shenzhen lab and lived there for two weeks. The last test was to run the equipment continuously for 72 hours in environments ranging from −10 to +55°C. At the end of the 72 hours, all of our little indicator lights were still burning steadily, and we knew that we had finally completed our toughest challenge. I still have fresh

The New Times Building, former home of Huawei R&D

Our R&D team, with an average age of under 30

memories of that day. I walked out of the plant at 5am in the morning on 12 May 2002 to find our Shenzhen campus looking more beautiful than ever before. The rays of the early morning sun lit up our scarlet, fan-shaped logo, and it shone like a beacon.

Later, Wei Leping, chief engineer of China Telecom, visited Huawei and spent a long time looking at our products. He said, "I would never have imagined that a world-class product like this was developed by a gang of young 20-somethings."

Never Forget the Core Strengths

One successful product is not enough to keep a whole department growing healthily. We were determined to build up a suite of core strengths, including chip development, technological innovation, and collaboration with external partners.

Buying chips from other vendors was pricey. With that kind of high cost base, we found it hard to make products that would deliver real value for money. So, from our very first generation of transmission products, we had been working on developing our own core chips. Even though we were still very understaffed, we kept some of our best people working on this problem.

At the time, He Tingbo (who is now the president of HiSilicon) was in charge of chip development. I was responsible for product development. A lot of the same instruments and meters are used to run tests for both products and individual chips, so she and I frequently got in each other's way as we sought out resources. Being a gentleman, I would always allow her to use the instruments first, but over the long term this was not sustainable. So, we came to a gentleman's agreement: she would have priority access during the day, and in the evening the equipment was all mine.

Our persistence and hard work paid off in the end. Our first generation of core chips was delivered just as we had hoped, and we went on to develop a series of chips that sold in the tens of millions. All this enabled us to build transmission network equipment that remained competitive and cost-effective over the long term.

One of the core technologies we are very proud of is our algorithm for automatically switched optical networks (ASON). In many countries, such as Brazil and India, fibre optic cables used to break frequently because of the difficult terrain, and that would cause the phone and internet signals to cut out. We designed ASON technology to deal with this problem. ASON is like satellite navigation for a network. Imagine that the fibre cables are the roads, and the phone or internet signal is a car. When one road is blocked, ASON will find a new route so that the signal can still get to its destination. When ASON was used in the networks of one Indian telecoms operator, its chief technology officer sent us this very satisfied comment: "Ever since we started using the ASON technology, there have been no communication outages due to broken fibre."

Huawei was also the first vendor in the industry to suggest and create end-to-end subnet management technology. Our technology offered an interface and smart routing. It made communications network maintenance very simple. By providing both software and hardware, we were able to significantly boost the overall competitiveness of our products.

At about that time, many countries were launching national broadband strategies and urgently needed efficient, flexible ultra-broadband fibre networks. We spotted the opportunity and piled on the pressure in our ultra-broadband R&D. That was how our switching equipment for optical transport networks (OTNs) came into being.

In the communications sector, before launching any new product, vendors must always consider the issue of interoperability with equipment made by other companies. Standards are the most common way in which this problem is solved. Huawei was the first company to make this kind of equipment, so one of the first issues we had to consider was how to update the relevant technical standards.

At the time, we were a new player. We had almost no influence on any of the standards committees. At the outset, the problem was not so much how to get agreement on our new standard. The problem was that the committee wouldn't even put the issue on its agenda. Soon, we realized that we could not win this battle by ourselves. We needed allies.

We sought help from China Mobile and China Telecom. They were already an influential voice in the global communications sector, and they were also looking to diversify and expand the industry. At a meeting of the China Communications Standards Association we were finally able to drive a thorough discussion of the OTN standard proposed by Huawei and, based on our customers' commercial imperatives, we hammered out how the standards would evolve. Then, we worked with our partners and customers outside China, delivering lectures and participating in workshops in global standards organizations. By that time, we had a strong set of arguments and materials to back up our position. We had powerful supporters. And the technology we were proposing was good: it was forward-looking, but backward compatible, and we had taken on board many different suggestions along the way.

Ultimately, we were able to evolve the standards, one step at a time. By the time the standards took shape, our proposals accounted for 75% of the content of the OTN standard. That gave us a strategic edge in the ultra-broadband optical transmission sector. Within three years, we developed the equipment, which supported a big jump in the sales for our fibre transmission products over the next few years.

But building up our core technical strengths was not something we could do entirely on our own. We needed to find help externally. In 2002, we got wind that a company named Optimight was for sale. This company specialized in long-haul wave-division multiplexing (WDM), one of the core fibre transmission technologies that we needed. So, we asked Huawei leadership for approval to acquire Optimight. The dot-com bubble had only recently burst and cash was very tight. The leadership had all taken pay cuts themselves. However, they thought the technology was promising, and they approved the acquisition.

This bold decision later came to be regarded as the best deal that our transmission networks team ever made. Thanks to the acquisition of Optimight, we managed to roll out our ultra-long-haul WDM solution in no time. This solution helped us quickly grow into a global market leader.

The selection of the right path also played a key role in building the company's core strengths. In 2005, we wanted to launch our own microwave transmission equipment. However, the microwave market was well served by established vendors, and there was no demand in China. It seemed that we would be forced to go head-to-head with experienced rivals in the international market.

At first, we wanted to start selling in the traditional microwave equipment market. However, we were not sure whether we could succeed in this market. During a visit to Vodafone, we were told there were already more than enough companies selling traditional narrowband microwave transmission equipment. However, they hadn't decided yet which vendor would get the opportunity to meet their next generation internet protocol (IP) microwave needs. These comments added to our determination to go all out to develop and sell microwave transmission equipment for IP networks. Subsequent events would confirm the wisdom of that decision.

Our IP microwave transmission team was bidding for the Vodafone project, but Huawei had no brand name in this field. Our front line sales staff and the team in R&D worked in close collaboration, 24 hours a day, guiding us through three rounds of tests and technical negotiations before we were able to make Vodafone sit up and take notice of Huawei's IP microwave offerings. This shifted Vodafone's perception of us, and their disbelief and suspicion gave way to gradual recognition of our strengths. In the end, we won the Vodafone contract. It made Huawei's name in this sector.

But our celebrations were short-lived. Vodafone demanded that we pass their admission tests within seven months. That put our R&D team under a lot of pressure. We were using a whole new set of chips and unproven technologies, but we were able to

Our products went
on to become a huge
success in the market,
and other operators
across Europe flocked
to build a relationship
with the Huawei
microwave team.

overcome all of the teething problems. Moreover, we made a forward-looking shift in the software architecture. Finally, during Chinese New Year 2009, when most people were home spending time with their families, the R&D team came together for a final push to get us through the Vodafone admission tests. Our products went on to become a huge success in the market, and other operators across Europe flocked to build a relationship with the Huawei microwave team.

We Will Conquer 100G

Now that we had mastery of the core technologies, and we had successfully created 2.5G and 10G products, we were ready to push on to new peaks of 40G and 100G. First, we made a bold push for 40G bandwidth. This placed our equipment in a class above any competitor's, and our 40G solution quickly became the new standard in Europe and other developed markets. Coupled with a new architecture that we launched for optical transmission networks, our WDM products for fibre transmission became the market leader in 2008. Even so, we didn't let up the pressure for one moment. We started focusing our R&D efforts on developing a solution that would operate at 100G.

Unlike our previous products, 100G represented a real leap beyond the existing state of the art. It was a real longshot. We gathered some of the top minds in fibre technology and drew on many interdisciplinary insights. Successful completion required the combined resources of Huawei and many external partners.

In November 2008, while our 40G product was still in the final stages of development, the Fixed Network Product Line set up a joint team to develop a 100G solution. The team was given the name '2091'. This team of several hundred members was scattered all over the world – it was a team on which the sun never set. Led by a core group of PhDs and industry experts, 2091 kept working 24 hours a day on a dash to victory. In terms of management, we made a lot of innovations for this team. We made sure that each of our expert contributors was given the respect and trust they deserved, so that they could all do the work that they had always dreamed of doing.

June 2011 was a defining moment in the story of our 100G project. Our chips were being fabricated in Japan but, on 11 March 2011, the Fukushima tsunami wreaked havoc on the entire country. As a result, our chips couldn't be shipped until 8 June. We were due to start services for our customer in the Netherlands, Royal KPN, on 15 June. Five days after that, the product would be officially launched at the IIR forum in Monaco. From shipment of chips to customer delivery, we had just seven days. No one thought we could make it.

"Even if we only have a 1% chance, we still commit 100% to getting it done" – that was the attitude of the entire 100G team. We were locked in a race against time. We developed a plan for fast product launch call 'Mt Emei', and went over and over every detail. We put in place contingencies for every risk. And we stationed top people at the manufacturing and assembly sites to make sure any problem could be spotted and instantly resolved.

On 13 June at 6.15pm, the Mt Emei Task Force boarded a flight from Japan to Hong Kong.

At 10.05pm, the Task Force arrived in Hong Kong and went immediately to the Huawei Shenzhen R&D facility. With 'Deep Sea', we executed the high-speed assembly and commissioning of the 100G solution.

On 14 June at 0.05am, 'Deep Sea' and 'Rich Soil' were successfully united.

On 14 June at 8.12am, every top specialist gathered in the opto-electronic lab and started preparation.

In the early hours of 15 June, we split into two groups – one headed for Amsterdam, the other for Luxembourg. However, when we arrived on-site at the customer premises, the equipment did not work. We had made a promise to the customer, and they were waiting with a billboard ready to unfurl, a press release ready to send out. You can imagine how much pressure there was on our shoulders at that moment. We still believed there would be a solution. The team in Shenzhen stayed online with us and gave us ideas on how we could address the issue. But the equipment had gone on strike, and nothing would conjure it back to life. We refused to give up and kept on eliminating possible causes one by one. We upgraded the software. The technical sales manager stood off to one side and received a call from the customer at 10pm. The customer was starting to worry. Were we actually going to be able to deliver this product or not? But all our hard work had not been in vain. At 11.30pm, the moment finally came when data began to flow through the new system. We all jumped for joy, our eyes brimming with tears of excitement.

On 20 June, as scheduled, Huawei and Royal KPN jointly announced Huawei's 100G solution at the IIR forum. More than 180 customers watched the presentation on how the equipment worked and saw data flowing in real time from the equipment on the networks of Royal KPN. At the conference, our KPN contact said, "Huawei has many very professional people with many years of experience. I hope that we can continue close collaboration with them in the future. We will invite our customers to observe

The 2011 IIR forum in Monaco

our 100G tests, because these tests are extremely important to our business." Orders for the 100G equipment poured in after the launch. In 2014, we made our first major sales in the Japanese and South Korean markets, which have the toughest technical standards in the world. Our business was really taking off.

We Never Stop

We have a special world map in our office. Every time we sell our equipment for transmission networks to a key account (i.e., a major telecoms operator), we stick a Huawei logo on the map. To date, we have delivered transmission solutions to more than 80 of the world's top 100 operators. These solutions serve more than 3 billion users and tens of millions of businesses, and connect millions of households. We are one of the world's most trusted transmission network providers. The rise of our transmission networks has also contributed to the boom in the communications market. In the early years, when only a few companies were able to deliver fibre communications solutions, the cost of rolling out a transmission network was very high. Our hard work has helped cut the cost of communications so that services are affordable for everyone.

Today, the demand for data is growing explosively, driven by 4K high-definition video and the upcoming 5G mobile networks. The convergence of information technology with communications technology means that we have an opportunity to roll out easy-to-operate networks that deliver a premium experience. Underpinning all of these new developments is fast data transmission infrastructure, and that is exactly what the transmission networks team delivers. So, for us, the market is huge. Afloat on these vast seas of data, we still have the same goal as we always did: to be a leader. But now, we are not content to lead just in terms of sales. Huawei wants to lead the industry.

We never slow down, never ease off, never stop pushing the limits.

Lightning Chasers

By Xiong Ying

I spent the entire summer of 1998 'putting out fires' with two other colleagues.

That summer, there were many thunderstorms and Huawei's equipment suffered major damage from lightning strikes. Lightning first hit the transmission products, followed soon after by an enormous quantity of switches and access equipment. As there was no dedicated team focused on lightning protection, we were assigned as provisional 'firefighters' to deal with the issues. Each day there was a new emergency that left us scrambling to catch up. On one occasion, during an emergency drill, I found myself rushing back to my room to grab my bags, the driver below desperately honking the car horn. I was in such a hurry to get back downstairs that I slammed right into a glass door. I broke my nose and smashed my glasses to pieces.

Upon arrival at the test site, as I held the burned board in my hands, I didn't have any tears left to express my despair. I did not have any understanding of the design and standards for lightning protection, so I was working completely blind. I might wriggle my way out of one issue, but would get caught by the next. I felt really bitter about things at the time, and I would mutter to myself: "Why is our lightning protection so outdated?"

Looking back on all of that now, it almost seems comical. There are many incredible stories to tell about how we moved from fearing and avoiding lightning to actively pursuing and guiding lightning.

The Best Forklift Driver on Staff

Prior to 1999, due to a lack of consideration for design, device DC power slots had weak protection against lightning and were thus highly susceptible to lightning strikes. As we had some experience, we installed lightning protectors on DC power slots, which helped to solve the issue temporarily. However, to eradicate the root of the problem, we had to form a dedicated team that could incorporate lightning protection into the product design stage. With a broken nose to indicate my experience, I also joined that team.

During our first meeting, only a handful of people sat in the expansive room and stared at each other: could the few of us new recruits really solve the issue of lightning protection in the major product lines at Huawei? Luckily, not long after that, several Huawei experts with more experience also joined the team, finally enabling us to unite as an effective operating force.

We didn't have much hard data at hand, let alone any online courses. All we could do was use our spare time to read books, study theories, and look up case studies. When we didn't understand something, we would seek out one of our supporting experts. If they couldn't address the issue, then we'd do more reading. We even called in one of China's leading experts in lightning protection in the communications industry, Liu Jieke. He was the best of the best in terms of field operations. We desperately wanted to snatch at every straw, in the hope that one might be able to save us.

After receiving training, the eight core team members were assigned to eight important products involving wireless, switches, and access networks. Each of us began our respective attempts to develop lightning protection circuits, dealing with different types of ports, and trying to match lightning protectors to different circuit designs. To decide whether or not the protectors were up to standard would require testing. It was then we realized that the company didn't have any instruments to simulate lightning strikes. So, how were we going to test our plans?

Finding the right instrument immediately became our most urgent task. We asked peers in the industry, having heard that what we needed might be in Guangzhou. We were going to have to move a huge equipment cabinet on-site for the testing. Trucks weren't allowed in the city during the day, so we had to wait until the small hours to enter Guangzhou from Shenzhen with our vehicle. If you were there, you would have seen a group of old men moving a huge cabinet weighing hundreds of kilograms, along with soldering iron, cables, and a pile of other tools, onto a truck and heading into the city. After we arrived at our destination, we still had to use a forklift to get the cabinet down and into the lab, because it was so heavy. We had to go through this process regularly over a period of several months. I quickly became an expert forklift driver and was known as such by my colleagues.

'Workaholics' on the Production Line

As soon as we started working in the lab, we implemented the plans we had pulled together through experience. But the first test revealed problems: the circuit plans we had prepared did not provide effective protection for the communications ports. This result was to be expected, since the materials we had referenced had not been written for communications equipment. There were sure to be differences, and we had to carry out the tests while also looking for the right circuits for the company's products.

To take the circuit plan validation as an example, based on our original estimations, we only installed a lightning protector on the lightning protection circuit. However, it was found to be inadequate right from the start. Luckily, we came prepared, and added another protector, then confidently went back to test again – only to be faced with failure once more. What was going on? I was getting worried by this point. If we couldn't figure it out on-site, then we'd have to head back to Shenzhen to make further preparations, which would mean the entire week had been wasted. I was adamant that we find a solution. Luckily, I was the one who had installed the lightning protection circuits, so I looked at them carefully again and realized an inductor – the component used in conjunction with the lightning protector to improve its performance – was missing. I quickly removed the thick copper wire from within the cabling and built an impromptu inductor right then and there, which significantly improved the lightning protection performance.

This approach, amazingly, worked. I was excited, but the inductor was flimsy and would wobble if the board was moved. It was a good interim solution, until we could improve on it in formal delivery production.

Delivery production is another story of blood, sweat and tears. Because a lot of equipment did not give consideration to lightning protection, boards did not provide space for such functionality. We thus had to instal lightning protection circuitry into a box, assembling this into a lightning protector. We issued an instruction manual to help technical service engineers instal the lightning protector onto the equipment. It was February 2000, and the thunderstorm season was just two months away. The problem was, the lightning protectors were still on the production line and hadn't been assembled yet.

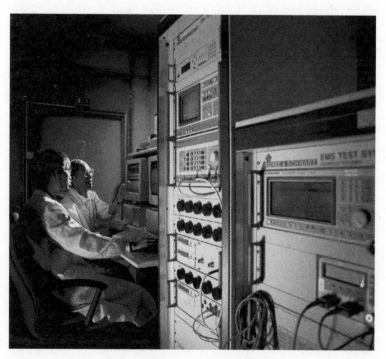

Tackling tough technical challenges

One day during a meeting, our boss, Chen Dunli, received a call from the Product Line informing us that the shipping date had been confirmed. They wanted to know where our lightning protectors were. Our boss became so animated that he slammed his hand down on the table and shouted: "Get me a car! We're going to the production floor ourselves!" I was flabbergasted: "What do you mean we're going to the production floor?" Before I had a chance to digest the situation, I found myself in a Shenzhen factory with two other colleagues and the boss.

No one knew the lightning protectors better than we did. We didn't need training before jumping right into our new roles. We sat on the production line, welding the lightning protection circuits into the boxes. The work wasn't technical, but it took us what seemed like forever just to get a single box finished. The workers around us finished four or five boxes in the same amount of time. I looked up at Chen Dunli and saw him carefully focused on the assembly work. He was more devoted to the work than anyone else, and didn't even stop for a meal. The factory manager was impressed when he saw us there: "You engineers really are workaholics, coming down here to work with us!" But after three or four days, it was clear that our individual efforts weren't paying off, and our arms and hands were hurting from the work. Nonetheless, by being there on-site, we gave the manufacturer some pressure, and they arranged for additional shifts to speed things up, which did push progress forward.

Once the lightning protectors were sent to field offices and assembled onto equipment, they did their job well. Damage caused to products from lightning strikes was reduced considerably.

A 'One Vs Many' Challenge

Having had a taste of how tough it was on the ground, we no longer wanted to just be putting out fires and patching leaks. We wanted to get involved in the earlier stages of product development and incorporate lightning protection into design from the very beginning. We were still the same old team, and each of us was assigned to a different product line to lend support.

When I say, "to lend support," I actually mean, "to spark conflicts and cause trouble." Each product line expressed their support for our request, but implementation was a problem. We had to prove our worth to the product lines.

Not long after taking on work relating to wireless product lightning protection, a new product that had been installed with a lightning protector was damaged during a lightning strike. The head of the product line was annoyed and questioned me: "Don't you have strict testing of the protectors? They seem to be useless. Why don't you get it right first, then come back and talk to me about involvement in early-stage design!"

When I got on-site to inspect, I found that the location of the lightning protector was entirely wrong. The grounding plan was also not appropriate, which was why it hadn't done its job properly to protect the equipment. Despite this, my explanation failed to win the trust of the product line: "Do you have any evidence to prove that? If we make the adjustments you are suggesting, do you realize how much that will affect the product engineering plan?"

Without having resolved the problem, I left dejectedly. This was no way to solve the issue. Perhaps a comparison might help persuade them? I thought I might present a series of differently configured lightning protectors and let the members of the product line team see for themselves whether I was right. I analysed the effects of the lightning circuitry in detail. After multiple adjustments and optimizations, I then sought out another expert to see if my train of thought was making sense. With over 40 pages of documentation, the wireless product line engineers were quickly convinced: "Oh! So it really is that problem!" They immediately joined me in convincing the product line leadership, and got down to work adjusting the product engineering plans.

However, that wasn't the end of the battle. During the course of plan execution, we had trouble reaching consensus with the product hardware and architecture teams. In terms of the architecture, I repeatedly emphasized that lightning protectors had to be installed inside the cabinet next to the board in order to be effective. But the architecture team couldn't comprehend this: "Just put it inside, there is only so much space there, it's not going to fit." "But if we don't put it in this location, the lightning protection performance will suffer." "Give us proof of that!" All I could do was shake my head and return to the lab and prepare a series of test results with the protector in different locations. I used those results to explain one step at a time to the architecture engineers and eventually was able to convince them. While implementing the plan, the entire process seemed to be fraught with one battle after another.

Finally, the properly installed lightning protectors showed their value during the stormy season, and rates of damage and loss were reduced to almost zero. The Lightning Protection Team's technical capabilities were finally recognized by the product lines.

Lightning Protection: Are You Willing to Play with Fire?

With the advent of distributed base stations, remote radio units (RRUs) were installed on towers to reduce signal loss and cut network construction costs. This presented challenges to size. Teams working in radio and power sources were all eager to push for their products to be part of RRU. However, our lightning protection circuits were too large and hindered the process of miniaturization. During one review meeting, an RRU architect said bluntly: "Everyone's circuitry is just barely squeezing onto the highway, and your lightning protection circuit is sitting in the middle of the road like a 1970s Buick sedan."

We didn't have much to say in our defence: lightning protectors hadn't seen any major breakthroughs in the past few years, so how could we achieve miniaturization? The team brainstormed again and again, analysing the feasibility of each possible component miniaturization. We eventually came up with seven potential designs. Unfortunately, each of these met with failure.

Ideas continued to fly, but then got quickly rebutted. The plan wasn't moving forward. Had we really reached the limit? "Perhaps we should give the GXX component a try?" This was a suggestion from Wang Qinghai, a key technical employee of the team. Using this component could achieve a circuit that was half the size of a traditional component, but there was a serious risk: other lightning protectors would automatically shut off after responding to the power surge from a lightning strike, thus ensuring that the RRU and the lightning protector itself were both protected. However, the GXX component took up all the energy of the lightning strike in order to protect the other equipment and circuits. The adjustment of its voltage was a major technical challenge. If the voltage was too high, the GXX component wouldn't protect against the lightning. If it was too low, it could erroneously respond to DC power and damage the protector and the RRU. More frustrating even than that was the fact that the voltage would constantly change based on the lightning strike.

When the manufacturers heard our 'striking' idea, they weren't even willing to entertain the possibility. "Let's just leave it for now and look into things more," they told me. Some of them even called us wishful thinkers: "This plan of yours is like playing with fire on your power circuit!" However, this was the most feasible of all of the 'impossible' plans. If this route wasn't possible, then our process of miniaturization had perhaps reached its limit.

Perhaps it is a technical intuition that I have gained over many years, but I never believe fate deals us an impossible hand. I decided to give my all and tried every single wave form of lightning strike, seeking to find the most appropriate voltage for various conditions through trial and error. As the 'elder' of the team, even though I had butterflies in my stomach, I didn't let it show. Otherwise, the younger colleagues under me might have lost faith. I carried my own weight, while also encouraging the younger experts: "The next wave is going to throw us onto the beach sooner or later. Just give everything you've got, and let fate handle the rest!"

We began to regularly look over our own work and ideas and make adjustments. The first was the component feasibility assessments, then the simulations, and then the design, and finally the sample units. In order to find the critical point, each time we validated an electrical performance parameter, we would test the voltage one volt at a time. With each adjustment, we had to re-optimize the design, change the circuitry, make new samples, and upend everything and start again. In this way, each round of design and sample creation lasted for a continuous two or three months.

Throughout this process, testing and validation were our constant companions. There were upwards of 50 or 60 components that had to be incorporated into each round of testing, and each component had to undergo at least ten simulated lightning strikes. After several months of testing, our ears felt like they were buzzing, and we felt hazy and dizzy. Generally, after a high-voltage lightning strike test, the buzzing in our ears would last until we went to bed that evening.

Each round of testing was conducted full of hope and met with disappointment. We spent a tortuously long time in this repetitive cycle. Finally, after six rounds of sample creation and testing, we found the optimal solution for all conditions.

In that instant, as I held the data in my hands, my throat felt constricted and I couldn't speak. The joyous scene I had imagined in my mind over and over again did not play out. But the size of our lightning protector was cut by half, and we left the competition in the dust, once again. We had done something no one else in the industry had dared to imagine.

Seizing Real Lightning

After the excitement had faded, we were surprised to discover that we had been pushed into what Huawei founder Ren Zhengfei likes to call 'uncharted territory'. With our new solution, it was no longer possible to rely on the lightning protection specifications we had used in the past. We had to find real lightning in order to obtain the most precise data. This was the only way for us to check whether the simulation modules were appropriate and accurate, and to further optimize the lightning protector.

But how could we 'seize' actual lightning? "Rocket-triggered lightning!" This daring idea was proposed by one of our teammates. It was something only three or four organizations were doing globally, and it was mostly for meteorological research or national defence. No one in the ICT industry had ever proposed doing it, but the data from this method was the most precise, and so it was irresistible to us.

In 2010, we met the Guangdong Provincial Meteorological Bureau, and this marked the start of our rocket-triggered lightning project. Pulling along the power and battery cabinets, several of us squeezed into the cabin of a truck and rode the whole bumpy way to the Outdoor Lightning Detection Base of the Chinese Academy of Meteorological Science.

Adjusting and testing the rocket-triggered lightning test equipment

The Outdoor Lightning Detection Base at the Lightning Protection Center of Guangdong Province – the weather forecast showed that the next day there would be thunderstorms, so we spent the night constructing an artificial lightning attraction environment

In our normal work, we were always worried about lightning strikes damaging our equipment. But now we found ourselves intentionally looking for lightning and realized it was tougher to find than we imagined. When we got word of the weather, we rushed to the location as quickly as we could, but the storm clouds had already passed when we arrived. We rushed back and forth between the base and the launch site countless times in a day. Sometimes we finally had the weather we were looking for, but then the rain was too heavy, and the test tower was at risk of being directly struck by lightning. This made it impossible for us to climb the tower to instal the test battery, so we again had to return empty-handed.

After chasing lightning for 18 years, we gradually transitioned from studying lightning protection products to studying lightning itself.

With all eyes on the calendar, we watched as the stormy season began to pass without giving us the opportunity we needed. The weather remained sunny and hot. On 3 September, there was light rain and I was waiting for the call as usual at 6am. Everyone had their eyes glued to the radar and electric field diagrams. By 8am, there still wasn't the right mix of conditions to trigger lightning. But, suddenly, the satellite cloud map showed a layer of cloud was about to pass over the base. The research staff from the Guangdong Provincial Meteorological Bureau called out: "Get ready to go!" We once again found ourselves blustering along the road to the base in the middle of a storm. A dozen or so of us were squeezed into the tiny 'Rocket Control Room', dripping wet and hearts fluttering between hope and discouragement, wondering which it would be that day.

We sat there for more than ten hours, staring intently at the radar and electrical field maps. At around 9pm, the intensity of the electrical fields in the cloud layer grew. "Prepare for launch! Three, two, one, ignite!" The rocket carved a path through the air like a sword being brandished from its sheath, heading towards the clouds. Suddenly, multiple blinding streaks of lightning shot down onto the tower, leaving us all awe-struck and lost for words. I don't know who shouted first, but after that everyone broke into cheers. We had finally captured lightning and successfully guided the electricity onto our communications tower, obtaining extremely valuable raw data. I had seen on television the expressions of joy of scientists working on rocket launch projects. At that moment, I also knew that incredible sense of joy.

After chasing lightning for 18 years, we gradually transitioned from studying lightning protection products to studying lightning itself. Today, whether it be torrential rain or thunder and lightning, the effects of such phenomena no longer cause major disturbances to everyday life. We are able to make calls to relatives far away and chat with friends by video across oceans.

Behind these everyday activities is our team and its tireless effort expended over a decade, never admitting defeat and always testing the limits of what is possible. As I bid farewell to my youth and look back on things, I can proudly say that I have no regrets.

This Code is Named After Me

By Gao Liang

Munich in early autumn always hints at cooler weather. I feel lucky each day as I travel to and from the Germany Research Center. In my tenth year at Huawei, and the best years of my life, I am able to work and study in one of the most developed countries in the world. It truly is a dream come true.

Without the platform that Huawei has offered me, I might not have had such a valuable opportunity. Without the open and inclusive environment that Huawei offers, as a regular old R&D staff member, I wouldn't have had such a wonderful space in which to grow and develop. I have so many memories through the expanse of my time with Huawei.

Little Program, Big Heart

In 2006, having just joined Huawei, I was part of the development team for the new Online Charging System (OCS) product. There were may internet services cropping up at that time, including video calling, web surfing, games, and other entertainment. A single charging model no longer met the needs of the rapidly changing telecoms market. There was an urgent need for a system that could charge users for the use of online resources in a real-time, accurate, and customized manner. This led to the development of OCS.

Our first customer was Guangdong Mobile. The customer demanded that, within two months, we ensure the OCS could generate detailed report data from the previous day every night. They wanted three reports, covering information such as user balance and changes in the status of users. The rules for data calculation were very complex. The project team originally took a practical approach, thinking that all that was needed was to write the code using the then-available target formats and rules.

However, upon more detailed analysis, I discovered a problem: the definition rules for some of the fields in the report were vague and required the confirmation of system engineers (SE) and the customer. This meant that the results of data compilation might not be accurate, and the process would also be labour-intensive. When the storage location of data changed, the code for report generation also had to be frequently revised. From a longer-term perspective, if business volume grew, what would happen when they needed a fourth, fifth, or even more reports?

I wanted to write a more flexible program that would not be restricted to mechanically generating the three reports currently requested by the customer. I wanted one that could generate any report based on inputted configuration.

I put together a two-month implementation plan and spent my spare time writing a prototype program to validate the feasibility of my idea. Even though developing such a program would be more difficult and time-consuming, my tests showed that it was feasible. So, I drummed up the courage to speak with the project manager (PM) about my idea. To my surprise, the PM gave me a very supportive response. However, we were very shorthanded at the time, and only one new employee, named Zhang Hehua, was available to work as my partner on the task. I told the PM that I didn't mind and I was sure I would be able to finish the work on schedule.

After that, I jumped into high gear, writing code, optimizing algorithms, and working with Zhang to test various scenarios. It would often be the middle of the night by the time I returned home after work each day. But, in the end, we managed to deliver a new program. While still satisfying the performance metrics laid out by the customer, the average cycle to develop a new report shrank from two weeks to one day. That was an impressive improvement in efficiency.

Later on, the number of reports requested by the customer did, in fact, increase from three to more than a dozen. But we didn't have to revise the main program. Instead, all we had to do was adjust the configuration documents. It was really gratifying to see my idea put into practice and become a reality. It felt like I'd developed a superpower; it was empowering and encouraging. Later, at other sites, staff could simply input configurations according to customer requirements. This reduced the need for back-and-forth discussions between field offices and R&D. It also saved on R&D costs, which further demonstrated the value of the program.

Someone asked me: "Why are you doing so much overtime and working so hard?" For me, even though it was perhaps just a tiny tool, it greatly improved the efficiency of our delivery. We face a lot of difficulties and challenges in life. I like to test what is possible, and I especially like to place higher demands on myself for work targets. I often find myself naturally seeking out the best solution, and am always willing to give more time and effort to achieve this goal.

Tiny Young Person, Big Award

"Gao Liang, this language programming you've done is impressive. You've tackled a major issue in delivery. We have to give the solution a name – how about we name it after you and call it Gao Liang Code?" These were the words of the R&D representative, Zhang Fan.

"You've got to be kidding, that's a bit over the top, don't you think? I don't want to be famous."

"It's not just my decision. The guys over in Product Line also agree. You're going to have to live with your newfound fame!" Zhang Fan smiled.

Not long after finishing the report module, I joined the development work for the principal OCS service. OCS offered a wide range of complex functions through data configurations. The volume of coding that was required had been greatly reduced, which enabled us to iterate faster. However, the enormous number of product deliveries resulted in many new customer demands. New problems emerged in the management of product versions when multiple people were involved in the configuration. For example, someone had to decide what the configurations would be, who would make the changes, what the reasons for doing so were, whose changes were right and whose wrong, and at which stages problems occurred. The management of these comparisons, combinations, revisions, and rollbacks demanded a lot of manual effort, and the efficiency of collaborative development was greatly affected.

How could we maintain the strength we had in data configuration while also retaining the mature version management in traditional code development? I lost myself in thought. After reading through extensive materials, I came up with the idea of using a more readable text format to redefine the configuration data. In R&D, this is what we call 'pseudo code'. This text format would be simpler and easier to understand than normal code. It would be more closely linked to business and would also offer various advantages for version management. In technical terms, it would be a 'domain-specific language'.

After we decided to do it, we jumped right into the work, and the team was very supportive of my idea. We initiated the Convergent Billing Development Environment (CBDE) project. After internal pilot applications began, the configuration model didn't change, but the domain-specific language addressed the issue of version management when there were multiple people collaborating in a large-scale configuration scenario. The changes were welcomed with open arms.

CBDE was then applied more widely. Previously, a team of 20 people simultaneously delivering to two or three projects of telecoms operator customers would be a tough task. But now we were able to deliver to eight or more projects, providing highly efficient support for delivery to multiple sites at the same time.

The company recognized me for my work, and named the new language after me with the name 'Glee' (taking my initials GL as the first two letters). As I mentioned earlier, the Chinese name was 'Gao Liang Code'. This was the first time the company had named software after a developer, which made it an even greater honour for me.

In November 2008, I attended a meeting for dedicated employees, marking the company's 20th anniversary, and received an

Individual Business Innovation Award. I would never have been able to reach such heights in the corporate world at the age of 25 without Huawei's inclusive and open environment.

Small Function, Big Effect

There is an old saying in China: "The prior generation plants the trees, and the next generation gets the shade." But, every now and then, you plant a tree and it grows fast enough to let you enjoy the shade as well.

In 2012, while participating in the development of the next-generation charging system, CBS5.5, I wrote several hundred lines of code to add an inconspicuous function to the system: after the system processed each charging request, it would automatically output a simple 'processing summary log'. This would only consume an additional 5% of performance, but would enable us to review our processing on the existing network at any time by opening the log.

In 2013, the CBS5.5 system was being prepared for launch in Bahrain. By this time, I was in charge of the team tasked with back-end release assurance work. This was the first site for CBS5.5 to be launched anywhere in the world and involved a dozen or so modules. It was do or die.

Several days after launch, a problem occurred. We discovered that a portion of balances of a small number of users had been 'frozen' and could only be restored through special processing. As only a few users had been affected, the small number of samples made it hard to track and analyse the problem.

The management of product R&D at all levels was very cautious with such a core module in the billing system, and no defects were allowed. The issue had to be identified and addressed as quickly as possible. As the team leader for assurance work, and one of the programmers for core modules, I was under considerable pressure. After we came up empty-handed using conventional methods of analysis, I had a flash of inspiration. My mind flew back to the tool I had programmed previously.

Tiny tools can have a
big effect. Sometimes
putting in that little
extra thought, or a
tiny bit more effort,
can really make a
difference at a
critical juncture.

I ran the summary log for an entire night and, after careful review, I managed to uncover some clues. Following the clues, I engaged in in-depth analysis and testing simulations with development and testing staff. It turned out that an external system linked with our charging system was not following standard protocols under a very specific circumstance. The sun was about to rise as we figured this out, and there was a palpable sense that a burden had been lifted from our shoulders. We quickly got down to working on a solution. But I still had a lingering sense of trepidation. If it hadn't been for this tool, I would have been in quite a pickle. It might have taken many more days before we were able to figure out what was going on.

I've spent many years working on OCS, from developing tools to handling core charging modules. I've participated in the development and technical improvements of major functions, and have received the company's Top 10 Module Design Engineer (MDE) Gold Medal Award. But that tiny tool that I programmed is something that has always stood out in my mind.

Tiny tools can have a big effect. Sometimes putting in that little extra thought, or a tiny bit more effort, can really make a difference at a critical juncture.

Small Event, Big Host

If you'll allow me to boast a little, I would say that I am the best coder in the hosting world, and the best host in the coding world.

I love programming and I also like to engage with people. I used to have a pet project I would think about often, which was that in the future, with so many programmers at Huawei, there should be a platform that enabled everyone to share their coding techniques, learn from each other, and 'duke it out' when need be. As I pondered this, I realized it might be fun to start a programming competition.

In my spare time, I wrote a 'Tetris' competition platform. Unlike similar competitions on gaming websites, the game

I designed was not a competition between people or between people and computer. Rather, it was a program-against-program competition. Competing programmers would program and develop plugins, and have the plugins battle it out on the gaming platform. It was kind of like an 'add-on', but it wasn't comparing the speed of execution in the game (which was, of course, faster than humans), but rather the algorithmic strategy.

This was right up the alley of programmers: even though I'm lousy at gaming, I can program like the best of them and, if we're competing in programming strategies, I might be better than you. The competitions were really fun to watch, and the programmers' techniques were innovative and interesting.

After the platform was launched, I first sent it to a few colleagues to test the waters. They were quickly hooked and began playing in their spare time. The game spread like wildfire and

Gao Liang (left) hosting a gaming competition

became hugely popular. Multiple competitions broke out between teams and between departments, everyone striving to become the platform champion.

In 2013, the platform officially took the stage at the Huawei Nanjing Research Center's 'Coding Talent Contest', with a competition carried out between departments. Because of the enthusiastic response, the platform was soon promoted to other research centres, and a number of competitions were held at university campuses in Nanjing. These activities attracted large numbers of very capable programmers, and we received many high-quality works.

In 2014, I released the second competition platform themed on the game 'Sokoban', a type of transport puzzle, in which the player pushes boxes or crates around in a warehouse, trying to get them to storage locations. Into this existing game, I incorporated rules that were more conducive to a programming competition. In 2015, my third offering was released, themed on the game Bomber Man. Slowly but surely, these competitions became a tradition at the Nanjing Research Center of Huawei.

At the annual competitions at research centres and universities, I, as the developer and organizer of the platform, shouldered the responsibility of a new role: host. In this role, I became known as 'The Famous Talk Show Host From Nanjing'. I guess I fit the role rather well.

As I like to say, every flower blooms, regardless of how big or small it might be. With such beauty all around, what is there not to be joyous about? Over the years, as I have followed OCS from its days as a new product to gradually obtaining the largest market share in the world, I too have grown from my days as a humble developer. From those simple beginnings, I have moved towards MDE, and the role of Chief Programmer. In 2015, thanks to my performance in the realm of domain-specific language, I was transferred to Huawei's Germany Research Center. There, I was put in direct contact with the most advanced theories and practices abroad. I was also given the opportunity to participate in design and actualization work for technology applications.

I am grateful for everything Huawei has given me these past ten years – such space to learn, grow, and constantly provide value and realize my potential. I am always sure that no matter where you find yourself at the moment, as long as you work your hardest, you will eventually see the light. Let's keep rockin'!

In Our Time

By Sun Cheng

The Huangpu River in all its majesty flows forever onward. On its shores, the historical buildings and soaring modern skyscrapers complement one another's radiance and beauty, and highlight the Shanghai skyline. About 20km away, an enormous glass-walled building stands tall and proud. This 880m-long office building is the equivalent of two 88-storey Jinmao Towers placed side by side. It has an area of 360,000m². Every working day, this 'Enormous Glass Box' attracts, with a seemingly magnetic force, tens of thousands of engineers. This is Huawei's Shanghai Research Center. The world's top talent in communications have been brought together here and work in world-class laboratories. Numerous products and solutions for the mobile communications field were brought to life here. But it's worth remembering that, 20 years ago, this enormous R&D centre was just a four-office site on Xietu Road in Shanghai's Xuhui District.

Holding One's Head High Despite Challenges

Wang Haijie was one of the first R&D employees to join the Shanghai Research Center. In 1997, when he was about to

A view of Huawei's Shanghai Research Center

finish his master's degree, he was most interested in working for Motorola. He says that, at the time, everyone involved in wireless wanted to work for Motorola. It never occurred to this young man that he would eventually choose Huawei. He certainly never expected that 15 years later he would be in charge of Huawei's largest research centre, overseeing a team of more than 10,000 R&D staff.

What changed the trajectory of his life was a chance encounter that summer. Several self-proclaimed Huawei R&D chief engineers found their way into the Shanghai Jiao Tong University residences and began talking with everyone: "If you want to be involved in core technology, why would you want to join a foreign company? Come join Huawei." This was the era in which China's mobile communications were transitioning from first-generation analog systems to second-generation digital systems. Huawei was preparing to establish a research centre in Shanghai, and wanted to leverage the talent in the city to engage in Global System for Mobile communications (GSM) R&D. In the early days, there were only seven or eight people, including Yang Ganghua, Zhang Jiemin, and Hu Xinyue. There was an urgent need to expand the team. So, Huawei turned to the outstanding talent studying communications at institutions such as Fudan University and Jiao Tong University.

"The telephone was invented more than a century ago, and yet our country has still not built its own communications industry. This generation of communications experts has to build GSM for China." This is what Yang Ganghua said to encourage everyone who cared to listen at the Shanghai Jiao Tong University student residences. Wang Haijie was inspired by this. Having studied communications for so many years, he was eager to do something of substance and joining Huawei suddenly seemed like the way to do it.

Wang Haijie told me about the day he reported to work for the first time at the Shanghai Research Center: "The office was on the third floor of a factory building. It was really dark and rundown in there. I was given a second-hand computer, and no one really got in my way. I was both excited and a bit lost. The materials next to me were piled to the ceiling, there were tons of new technologies and I had more things to learn than time in the day."

On the day he reported for work, he happened to meet Yang Ganghua and Zhang Jiemin, who were carrying boxes of materials from Shenzhen HQ. These R&D big shots in Shenzhen and Shanghai got down to work on their GSM journey. They read through GSM communications principles, plowed through protocols, carried out testing, and hunted out niche reference documents. On the hottest days of summer, the team could be seen, shirtless, in the lab commissioning and testing. In the mornings, they would rinse themselves off using the restroom sink. When tired, they would lay out a mat and sleep on the ground wherever they found themselves. The building's security guard was even heard saying: "What sort of company is this? Why are there all these labourers lying about on the ground all the time?"

They studied day in and day out, pursuing agile development and achieving rapid progress towards their goal. In September

The former location of the Shanghai Research Center:
Haiwen Business Building on Xietu Road

1997, integrated testing for GSM began. Because the early-stage development had been overly hasty, many problems arose in the final stages. At one meeting on integrated testing, someone asked Yang Ganghua whether he was confident in getting the job done. Yang Ganghua replied, brimming with confidence: "This knowledge-based work is something we can do just as well as anyone else."

China's Own GSM

Then came 24 October 1997. On this day, Huawei's GSM product was unveiled during the P&T/EXPO COMM CHINA in Beijing. The equipment had arrived in Beijing three days earlier, and the participating R&D staff had also arrived early to get things ready. There was both excitement and nervousness in the air, as we worried that our product would not work.

Sometimes it seems the more you worry about something, the more likely it is to happen. While attempting to connect Huawei's equipment to the public network, problems arose. The team worked from morning to night commissioning and testing and the system still wasn't working. The next morning was the start of the expo and everyone felt the pressure mounting. The team wasn't even in the mood to eat. But, in the end, the problem was found to be a simple issue with parameter configuration and, after some adjustments, the trouble was cleared up.

The next day, during the expo, the red banner above the Huawei booth proclaiming 'China's Own GSM' was eye-catching. Representatives from provincial telecom operators, competitors, and government departments were swarming around in front of the displays. They couldn't believe that Huawei had been able to develop a full set of GSM products in such a short period of time, and were using instruments to carry out all sorts of tests. Huawei's demonstration of GSM products had suddenly become the talk of the industry. After this, the market price of products from Western manufacturers dropped significantly in China. Over three years, beginning in 1998, the price declined by a full 80%.

At the time, everyone thought that the gates of success had been blown wide open. It seemed certain that Huawei's GSM solution would become the company's second engine of growth and a major pillar product. Who could have known that this was only the first step in the journey?

In the mobile communications market, it is generally the case that if you can 'fence off' a piece of the market, then you will succeed. China's 2G systems were far behind those of Western countries, and China's market territory had already been captured by major international companies, such as Motorola and Ericsson. The GSM solution that had come so late to the game thus had trouble gaining traction and wasn't going anywhere fast.

Beginning in Rural Areas, then Expanding into Cities

Living to see another day is what matters most. In and around the year 2000, Huawei was surviving on the scraps between the cracks in the market. The company began to redefine its market positioning for GSM by turning its attention to the larger rural market and other peripheral regions. At that time, China's medium and large cities already had networks deployed by large Western communications companies. The remaining peripheral and rural regions were not a focus of their attention, and many people were travelling to the cities to buy a phone and then returning back to the countryside to find it couldn't be used there.

GSM was positioned to serve this market. Huawei designed a competitive product – a peripheral network mobile that was small in size, low in cost, and quick to deploy. The solution could address communications coverage issues for telecom operators in rural areas. At this time, when a rural network was put through, often the operator would set up a table in the town square and residents would line up to register for a phone number. Huawei's presence was palpable throughout the less-accessible parts of China.

Wang Qihua was a hardware design engineer working on small mobiles at that time. He has strong memories of his time climbing and inspecting the towers in rural areas. One day, when returning from an inspection, he got caught in a heavy rainstorm. As he drove down the mountain road, his car got covered in mud that kind of looked like peanut butter. Even though he was driving very slowly, when he came to one particularly steep slope, his car began to slide, and braking wasn't doing any good. "I was scared to death, but thankfully the car came to a halt on the side of the road closest to the mountain. The experience gave everyone quite a fright," he said.

Even though the conditions were tough, this approach of beginning with the edge network market in rural locations, and then expanding to cities, enabled GSM to gain some footing in the market during its early days. From villages to county towns, and from county towns to city districts, Huawei's business gradually expanded. It was precisely this sort of 'flower planting' through constant deployments and breakthroughs that enabled Huawei to open up the national markets for GSM of China Mobile and China Unicom. At the same time, GSM also saw a series of breakthroughs in developing nations in Asia, Africa, and Latin America.

Deploying an edge network in Lishui, Zhejiang, in 2001

Positioning Determines Our Position

By 2006, after several years of hard work, GSM had been deployed to a considerable scale, with growth doubling three years in a row. It gradually became the main product for the wireless division and even the company.

But, just as the company was starting to feel it might be able to let off the gas a little, one of the biggest crises ever to hit GSM arose.

In response to the market expansion by Huawei, industry competitors were also increasing investment and continually launching new products. These were more competitive than Huawei's offerings in all respects, including cost, functionality, and performance. GSM product functionality and performance were becoming increasingly seen as lagging behind the competition, and many projects globally were failing in the face of fierce market conditions.

"Positioning determines our position. In the past, GSM's long-term target has been to be a second- or third-tier offering. The result has been that we have provided third- and fourth-tier products. We are our own worst enemy. The height of our aspirations determines where we end up. If we're going to try, let's aim for the top!" said the Wireless Product Line president, Richard Yu.

In late 2006, we began the development of a product that would change the fate of GSM – the dual density base station. GSM Product Line president He Gang said: "We have to lead the industry in competitiveness, and this is how we can help GSM turn the situation around."

In Tower 9 of Huawei's Shanghai Research Center in the Lujiazui Software Park, the lights of the GSM offices were never out. Taxi drivers in the city were well aware of the working hours at Huawei, and would line up outside the gate at 10pm every night.

From the development director, product development team (PDT) manager, and version manager to the ordinary employee, everyone had dedication engrained in them and was determined to

Today, Huawei has
quietly become one
of the world's largest
suppliers of GSM
by volume, and the
company's GSM
products are used in
125 countries, serving
more than 1 billion
users worldwide.

push forward. After half a year of tireless effort, both day and night, the new dual density base station product was launched on schedule. The leading architecture and performance gave GSM products a leg up, enabling Huawei to quickly gain a competitive advantage.

In the first half of 2007, China Mobile chose Huawei's GSM offering to replace all its existing base stations in the centre of the city of Chengdu. The Super Product Development Team (SPDT) manager, Cao Ming, led a key project assurance team in the successful delivery of the project. The outstanding network quality was sufficient to prove that GSM had developed to the point where it could be deployed to any network around the world.

In early 2008, European telecom operator Telefonica/O2 awarded a project to Huawei involving GSM migration and capacity expansion of the network in Germany.

On 8 May 2008, Huawei collaborated with China Mobile to reach the peak of the world: Huawei's GSM base station, at an elevation of 6,500m, successfully transmitted images of the Olympic flame reaching the peak of Mount Everest for the first time.

Today, Huawei has quietly become one of the world's largest suppliers of GSM by volume, and the company's GSM products are used in 125 countries, serving more than 1 billion users worldwide.

A Decade of Honing the Sword

In the 1990s, while still in the tough days of catching up in the 2G field, Huawei was already turning its gaze towards 3G. The company hoped to keep pace with the industry and gain a more advantageous footing in the 3G era.

Zhou Hong, a product manager of the 3G base station, Bian Honglin, a 3G research manager, and others have recalled that, in the two years from 1998 to 2000, we completed everything – from equations, to model simulations, to key technology verification. At the time, the team reported that somewhere around 200 people would be needed and a product could be completed within three years. In reality, eight years later a total of nearly

2,000 people were involved, equivalent to half the company's workforce at the time. If the size of the investment had been known, it's an open question whether the company would have been so willing to persevere.

In 2000, one of the landmarks in Shanghai, the Jin Mao Tower, became the work site of Huawei's equally landmark 3G team. More than 1,000 experts from Shenzhen, Beijing, and Shanghai converged on the sixth floor of the building, bringing with them eight brand-new devices, including 3G devices, base stations, and controllers.

In 2001, the entire network solution was launched successfully, and Huawei released its own 3G products in step with industry leaders, thus becoming one of a handful of manufacturers that was able to provide a full series of commercial systems. This time, it seemed that Huawei could finally enjoy the fruits of past efforts.

But reality is never so simple. Just as everyone was celebrating the success they had achieved and thinking big thoughts about the future of 3G in China, the global IT bubble popped in the telecom industry. Layoffs became the norm and the release of 3G licences in China was postponed. After about three years, Huawei's 3G business essentially had nothing to show for itself.

"Back then we were praying every day for China to issue 3G licenses. In 2000, when we were doing product planning, we thought they'd be released in 2001. Then, in 2001 we thought it would be 2002, and then we began hoping for a release in 2003. Upwards of 1,000 R&D staff were waiting every day for word, which meant an expense of more than ¥3 million. Everyone was really eager to know what would happen," recalled Wan Biao, the 3G R&D manager.

During the same period, several of China's telecommunication manufacturers were making good money from their investment in the Personal Access System (marketed in China as 'Xiaolingtong'). In the face of enormous pressure to turn the company's focus towards that market, Huawei's decision makers stuck to their guns and insisted that 3G represented the mainstream trend moving forward. They maintained their large investments in 3G. Over the course of several years, the R&D costs and expenses for several thousand staff amounted to billions of yuan.

One year, two years, three years ... it seemed as though 3G didn't have a hope in the domestic market. In order to survive, wireless staff were being forced to transfer to overseas markets.

The Secret Weapon that Turned the Tide

Wang Tao, a product manager, was among the first group of experts to expand wireless 3G markets overseas. "It was so tough to sell 3G. Western telecom vendors had a tight grip on the market, and they weren't leaving much room for us to breathe."

Wang Tao later became the president of Huawei's Wireless division. Thinking back on the early market expansion efforts, he told me: "We would dream about winning an order. We would clamour to seize any opportunity that popped up. At the time, CEO Ren Zhengfei was also really anxious. Any time he heard about a 3G project someplace, he'd fly straight there."

By the end of 2003, Huawei had finally been graced with some good luck. The company won a project to deploy a 3G network for Etisalat in the United Arab Emirates. This project was a lifesaver for Huawei. After several years of major investments, wireless 3G products were finally able to achieve a preliminary breakthrough.

A greater turnaround occurred a year later when, at the end of 2004, Huawei submitted a bid to build a 3G network for a small telecom operator in the Netherlands. During discussions, it was found that site costs were too high due to site leases and engineering construction. The operator urgently needed a solution that could go with cost-effective equipment rooms and rapid deployment.

Wireless Product Line president Richard Yu worked in the field with project members to survey sites and discuss plans. Through the on-site surveys and continual exchange of ideas, the team came up with a bold idea – to use distributed base stations.

In other words, they would divide the base stations into smaller components, like individual air conditioners. The base stations could be as small as DVD players, and the majority of functionality could be moved outdoors.

However, the work from thinking up the plan to implementing it could not be completed overnight. The team turned a regular meeting room in Tower 2 of the Lujiazui Software Park into a temporary office. Wu Wangjun, the lead designer for the plan, led key employees engaged with algorithms, hardware, and software. They moved their offices into that meeting room, carrying out design and development while discussing details.

Meng Qingfeng was one of the youngest staff members of the algorithm team. A decade later, he still had vivid memories of the intense technical discussions they had during that time, including how to connect circuitry and how to link up optical modules. How could reliability be achieved? What considerations were needed for heat dissipation and safety of hardware? Known as 'Boss Wang' by the team, Wu Wangjun lived up to his name. He was extraordinarily resolute in pushing to achieve an innovative solution, sometimes even overbearing when push came to shove. Each time a technical discussion was held, he would state bluntly: "We are not leaving until the plan is confirmed. Anyone who disagrees on the technical points is required to stay behind for further discussion."

A year later, what the industry was calling an 'architecturally disruptive innovative product' was realized at the Shanghai Research Center based on our original plans. Compared to traditional base stations, distributed base stations can be as small as one-tenth the size, and they can be as light as 1/15 the weight. All components can be carried by hand to the site, and project deployment is not as time- and labour-intensive.

In July 2006, because of the unique value offered by its distributed base stations, Huawei won a major share of a 3G network deployment project for Vodafone in Spain. This opened the doors for further business in Europe, and also provided a foundation upon which to further develop markets in Latin America, Eastern Europe, and the Asia Pacific region. In 2009, Huawei won a major stake in a China Unicom project involving 3G deployment. That year also marked the tenth year of Huawei's investments in 3G, and profits began to accumulate.

While achieving enormous success with distributed base stations, R&D teams did not relent in their innovative research to make base stations smaller, with greater bandwidth and higher performance. "If we're going to move beyond the fluctuations and passive situation we faced in the 2G era, we've got to have revolutionary solutions and products." In 2006, Lv Jinsong, a top expert in the radio frequency (RF) field and a Huawei Fellow, led the RF algorithm team in seeking to overcome the challenges faced globally in GSM multi-carrier technology.

By late 2007, Lv Jinsong led a multi-carrier project team in Lab 903 at the Shanghai Research Center in Lujiazui. In collaboration with algorithm experts at Huawei's Russia Research Center, they spent one and a half years striving to achieve a breakthrough in GSM multi-carrier technology. Not long after that, the SingleRAN solution based on that technology was born. Through complex algorithms, this solution could achieve major reductions to telecom operators' investments by integrating 2G, 3G, and 4G standards in one single base station. This provided major new impetus to the communications industry and could certainly be termed revolutionary in nature. In one stroke, the breakthrough set the stage for Huawei to gain a strategic advantage in wireless.

In 2008, as part of the project for Telefonica O2 Germany, Huawei successfully delivered the world's first 2G/3G integrated SingleRAN network. In 2010, SingleRAN became an industry standard. In 2013, Huawei won three new major contracts for 4G in China, laying a foundation for Huawei to command a leading industry position in the 4G era. In 2014, Huawei's wireless business was at the forefront of the 4.5G/NFV industry and achieved an incredible transformation – from building products to building an industry.

A view of Huawei's Shanghai Research Center

Embarking on Another Journey

In October 2010, during the Shanghai World Expo, Huawei achieved a major feat for itself: the completion of the new location for the Shanghai Research Center, on Xinjinqiao Road in Pudong. Fifteen years after the founding of the Shanghai Research Center, its 8,000 staff finally moved to their long-awaited new home base.

In the same year, Huawei as a whole was undergoing a low-key but significant strategic adjustment. In the face of the future digital tide, the company had confirmed its enormously influential device-pipe-cloud strategy. Incorporated in this effort were Huawei's three main business groups: the Carrier BG (Business Group), Enterprise BG, and Consumer BG. As the research centre for flagship devices, the Shanghai Research Center witnessed the transformation and rise of Huawei mobile phones.

In fact, back in June 2004, the wireless team had established a mobile phone development team at the research centre, composed of 3G testing staff and a portion of platform personnel. At the end of 2004, through incubation and development, the company's mobile phone business was split off from the wireless product line to operate independently. However, during this period, the sales channels for mobile phones were essentially telecom operators. Even though some sales volume was recorded, the brand influence in the device market was very minimal.

In 2011, with guidance from the company's adjusted strategy, Huawei mobile phones shrugged off the white-label approach and took steps to enter the global mobile phone market. During the same year, Richard Yu assumed responsibility for the device business. Richard Yu is famous for being an intrepid leader. "For so many years, people at Huawei have known that we have to be first. There's no room for second place," he said. "Under my charge, Huawei devices will either meet their demise or see success. There is no third way."

What gave Richard Yu so much faith in success was Huawei's culture of dedication and the substantial R&D capabilities the company had developed in wireless communications over several decades. For example, at the Shanghai Research Center where Huawei's flagship mobile phones were researched and developed, there were eight large network/device laboratories, including the largest and most comprehensive electromagnetic compatibility lab of any mobile phone manufacturer, a laboratory used to test heavy user traffic with 6,000 real devices, and the most advanced voice laboratory. Behind every Huawei mobile phone is a world-class R&D centre and laboratory facilities.

Actions Speak Louder Than Words

In 2012, the Ascend P1, a product born at the Shanghai Research Center, kicked off Huawei's releases of high-end devices.

In September 2014, Huawei's Mate 7, the product that really laid the foundation for Huawei's position in the high-end mobile phone market, was completed at the Shanghai Research Center. The design of the phone gave it the industry's largest screen proportions. An all-metal body, fingerprint recognition, one-touch unlock, and other innovative features ensured the Mate 7 had a dazzling release. Sales were impressive across every market and the company struggled to keep up with demand for the product.

The 10-metre dark room laboratory

The greater the legend, the more hard work is sure to have gone on behind the scenes. As the Mate 7 product lead, one staff member named Long recalled: The R&D team gave their blood, sweat and tears to make this mobile phone a reality. They remained dedicated to excellence throughout the development process. We asked ourselves many questions, including: How could we solve the antenna performance issues that came with having a metal body? How could we make the fingerprint recognition the best possible? Where was the balance between having a big screen, a large-capacity battery, and a compact device body? In the face of so many issues, the R&D team liked to joke that it was like whack-a-mole: they would take care of an issue here and then an issue would crop up somewhere else. The various challenges were not only a test of the team's capabilities, but also their courage and willpower.

The head of the Product R&D Department, named Ping, noted that prior to the Mate 7, there were actually multiple different product solutions. After countless product R&D meetings, discussions, and investigations, the team gradually cut away product solutions. These solutions were always the result of complete devotion on the part of the R&D team but, if any small detail wasn't up to standard, then it would be adjusted. If there were still outstanding issues, then everyone would go back to the drawing board once again.

On the presentation screen each solution looked brilliant, but behind the scenes there was thankless effort and long hours of dedication. Structures would be adjusted for a 0.1mm change in size. Designs would be upturned to address a 1/10,000 chance of failure. It was precisely this sort of obsessive pursuit of excellence that enabled this mobile phone to achieve an enormous leap forward in product design. Whether it was in terms of appearance, hardware specifications, or user interface, there were major improvements all around. This was a true breakthrough product.

"In the very changeable mobile phone market, the pursuit of excellence and constant innovation were the only ways to create a product that would satisfy the needs of consumers," version manager Wang said. "We were constantly traversing new peaks and constantly beholding new vistas. We were in our element."

In April 2016, Huawei's latest flagship mobile phone, the P9, was officially released. This phone was the first collaboration between Huawei and the century-old German brand Leica, bringing mobile photography to the next level.

Five years prior, there wasn't a single Chinese brand on the global smartphone market. Five years on, Huawei was ranked among the top three mobile phone brands in the world, behind only Apple and Samsung. "Our goal of sales revenue in the coming five years is US$100 billion. The employees working on Huawei devices have never shrunk from a challenge. Our lofty aspirations mean that the road we're taking is sure to be extraordinary," said Richard Yu. As the centre of research for Huawei's high-end mobile phones, Shanghai is sure to be part of the effort to make all of this a reality.

Reaching for the Sky

In the financial district of Shanghai's Lujiazui, amid the forest of skyscrapers, a tower-shaped building is particularly eye-catching. This is the Jin Mao Tower, one of the tallest buildings in China, and once the location of Huawei's Shanghai Research

Center. A decade or so ago, when I first took a business trip to the Shanghai Research Center, I had trouble finding the entrance to the office section of Jin Mao Tower. The security officer said: "You must be with Huawei, right?" I felt a bit smug at the time, thinking that Huawei must be very well known. Later, I realized that the workers at Jin Mao Tower were all outfitted in formal business suits. Only Huawei staff were in shorts and flip-flops, which made them instantly recognizable.

Today, I still travel regularly for business and every time I take a taxi to the Shanghai Research Center and tell the driver to go to Xinjinqiao Road, the driver will also ask: "You must be from Huawei, right?" This building, the longest single-structure building on Xinjinqiao Road, has become a well-known high-tech landmark in Shanghai. The Shanghai Research Center has a glorious history of more than 20 years, and this has created a sort of legend – from four offices in a rundown factory to a 360,000m^2 R&D building; from having only several English protocols to business involving over 10,000 R&D staff engaged in networks, devices, and chips; from being a follower in the 2G era to becoming a challenger in the 3G era, a leader in the 4G era, and a pioneer in the 5G era. Behind the legend there are several generations of dedicated individuals. One generation of young people after another has passed the flame onward. They have carried the desire to change the world and have never wavered in spite of countless setbacks. They have constantly explored, innovated, expended patient effort towards breakthroughs, and slowly but surely made their dreams a reality. As a classic song in China titled *In Our Time* goes, "The flows of time, they change us." But we are also changing the world and spending the time of our youth without regrets.

Just as the waters of the Huangpu River never stop flowing into the ocean, unseen digital flows keep surging forth. In this enormous building in the northeast corner of Shanghai, dedicated engineers continue with their work with quiet effort. They are working to build a better-connected world.

Huawei Built a Research Lab for Me

By Renato Lombardi

A New Chapter in a Long Career

One day in late 2007, Denis Han from Huawei's microwave team (who was later appointed director of the Milan Research Center) called and asked me to meet him.

I had first heard about Huawei three years earlier, when I was working for Siemens, and we sold Huawei some microwave equipment for a project they were doing in Cambodia. Soon afterwards, I had the opportunity to visit Huawei's headquarters in Shenzhen, the exhibition hall in the F1 building, and the manufacturing centre. I was briefed on Huawei's history and my first reaction was: "This is not just a Chinese company." Huawei had very few people working on manufacturing, but R&D staff made up a huge proportion of its workforce, so Huawei could focus on long-term innovation and development. After I came back to Siemens, I delivered an internal report telling everyone that, though Huawei was still small as a multinational company, we would see a lot from it in the next few years.

That brief encounter with Huawei was like a first date, which ultimately led to my happy marriage with Huawei. However, I didn't have any further contact with the company until I got the phone call from Denis Han.

The meeting took place on Christmas Eve, at a café in Milan. Alex Cai, who was the director of the European Research Center, came along to interview me. But, instead of a job interview, it was more like a business planning meeting. Alex talked frankly. He said that Huawei was not yet able to manufacture the outdoor units (ODUs) that were the centrepiece of the company's suite of microwave products for IP networks. The products they were importing were not competitive, and they lacked talented people. They were looking for microwave experts to help them develop their own ODUs and identify where microwave was moving. The company was committed to becoming a competitive player in IP microwave and turning Huawei into a microwave brand name.

We spent the whole afternoon talking, and we agreed that Huawei needed to establish its own microwave R&D competence centre. And the centre should be built where there were a large number of talented people, who were the key to success.

Everyone had the same idea: Milan. As we all know, Milan is the home of microwave. Many famous companies – such as Siemens, Alcatel-Lucent, and Ericsson – have R&D and sales departments there. There are also universities, like the Polytechnic University of Milan, which specifically train people in microwave technology. So, we could benefit from the local resource pool and a complete ecosystem of companies, schools, and research institutes.

We even discussed the outlines of a plan: how many people, how much money, how much time, and so on. That meeting really excited me, and I finally made up my mind to quit my job with a Western company and go to work with Huawei. I knew that I would perhaps be in a lower-level position at Huawei, and it would be very difficult to leave a familiar place and start over

Renato Lombardi at the opening of the Microwave R&D Competence Center

again without my existing relationships and resources. But I have always seen myself as a man of passion, ready for new challenges. I could start a new life at Huawei, build my own team, and try new things. What could be more exciting than that? It would be a sort of rebirth, like closing one chapter and opening a new one. (My name Renato means rebirth in Latin.)

'Cutting Corners' and Starting with a Bang

We had an interesting time building the Microwave Division.

In the summer of 2008, a group of five people assembled in a small office in one corner of the Huawei Milan office, right next to the coffee machine. There was Denis Han, Logos Tao (who was the ODU PDT manager of Xi'an), William Gou, Franco Marconi, and me. The air conditioner was broken, and the office was noisy. But we envisioned our future there: renting an office, hiring the right people, and building a competence centre from scratch. It was this vision that kept us going through the boiling summer.

I made use of every opportunity and all my resources to let people in the microwave communications industry know about Huawei and the resources it was putting into microwave. I first sought out former colleagues who were all microwave experts with 10 or even 20 years of experience. We knew and trusted each other, and this was how I formed the original core team.

While we were establishing the competence centre, Huawei was facing critical business challenges. In October 2008, after Huawei won the bid for Vodafone's project, we came under great pressure to develop products fast. Vodafone requested that we deliver a prototype that could pass their proof-of-concept test within just a few months.

I prepared to build a test environment with my Chinese colleagues. But where should it be? The new offices in Milan were only just finished, and there were no laboratories yet. Huawei already had a mobile innovation lab in Spain, so most of my colleagues preferred Spain. But I insisted on doing the testing in

Milan, because I wanted to show the customer how committed and competitive Huawei's microwave expert team in Milan was. I thought that was the way to build a long-term relationship with the customer. In the end, we succeeded in establishing a joint innovation centre in Milan.

What I did next was a little irregular, but it's better to ask for forgiveness than permission. I had lunch with some customers at Vodafone whom I knew very well, and I asked them: "Next week, you'll have an official meeting with Huawei. Please ask Huawei to do the testing in Milan." A week later, the Vodafone account team came and told me, "Renato, you may not know, but Vodafone said they want us to do the tests in Milan."

I was very excited to hear this news. However, much to my surprise, the customer set the date for the proof-of-concept test as the day before the Chinese Spring Festival (25 January 2009). There were only a few weeks left, so we had to build the lab very quickly.

Hu Bin, the testing engineer, brought over a dozen of people from China to help us. I remember that I spent one weekend working as a carpenter and labourer, laying the tiles in the lab, along with the other Italians on the team. We did things that researchers don't normally do, such as flooring and wiring. We saw the Microwave Division as our home, so everyone was very committed. We knew this was a pivotal moment and we had to start with a bang. Everyone was so dedicated that no one had a problem coming in during the weekends.

We managed to build the lab from scratch within two weeks. But the deadline for the test came before the product had got to the important TR4 milestone.

Our Chinese colleagues in Xi'an and Chengdu gave up the chance to spend the holidays with their families so as to support us 24/7. Every day, after conducting the tests for the customer, the teams in Milan, Xi'an, and Chengdu worked into the small hours to identify problems and make improvements, modify the code and compile new versions, and conduct many rounds of tests and verification.

When faced with
two options,
sometimes you
have to start laying
the groundwork in
advance, instead of
waiting till the last
minute to make
a choice.

Renato Lombardi demonstrates innovations to a customer

That was when I came to realize the true meaning of dedication (*fendou*) and the values that inspire everyone at Huawei to keep forging ahead.

The tests hit a few roadbumps, but thanks to the concerted efforts of all the teams, we finally reached the customer's required standards about two weeks later. A few days after, Ryan Ding, the then-president of Huawei's Fixed Network Product Line, came to Milan. I explained to Mr Ding why we chose to do the test in Milan, but I was a little bit worried, because I had cut some corners. He said: "Don't worry. Because of your involvement, Huawei had decided to do the test in Milan – even before you asked. And it proved to be the right decision."

This was just the beginning, but it meant a lot to us. This was the first time we had demonstrated Huawei's own microwave technology to a key customer. We proved to the customer that Huawei Milan possessed not only R&D and design capabilities, but we also had technical sales and services capabilities, and were able to build relationships with customers. We deeply understood and met the customer's needs and delivered on them.

When faced with two options, sometimes you have to start laying the groundwork in advance, instead of waiting till the last minute to make a choice. Actually, Italians don't mind cutting corners, just like the Chinese: if there is an obstacle, I just go around it to reach my target. If we are absolutely forced to meet the obstacle head on, then we just try our best to overcome it.

A Two-Year Challenge Completed in One Year

By the second half of 2008, the Microwave Division in Milan had already taken shape. The in-house R&D of ODUs was then brought to the table.

Our ODUs were made by a partner company, and they were not competitive in terms of performance, technology, and overall quality. They didn't match up to the offerings of incumbent manufacturers in the field. Drawing on my more than 20 years of experience, I proposed a solution of just a single board during my first trip to our research centre in Chengdu. This solution would raise our performance and production capacity compared with the two-board designs offered by our competitors. But it would also increase technical difficulty, putting more pressure on our R&D teams.

Some people supported this new solution, but others didn't. My team members and I strongly believed in this solution, and tried to persuade other teams to go for it with us. After a long period of phone calls and emails back and forth, I decided to fly to Xi'an (because the Xi'an Research Center was just approved to be the new home of ODU development in China) to talk face-to-face with the R&D team of the Wireless Network Product Line.

It was a freezing cold morning. A few people, including Logos Tao and myself, wandered along the ancient city walls in the chilly wind for a long time. As we walked, we tried to analyse the strengths and weaknesses of both the old solution and the new one. I said to Tao, "We are confident that we can build this new solution. The industry doesn't believe that Huawei can make an ODU prototype within two years. We will prove to them that we can do it in one year."

Our discussion lasted a good four hours. Though we all knew that there was some risk in taking this new technical path, we insisted on our choice.

About a year later, in 2009, we succeeded. We built an ODU prototype and officially released our own microwave product. My team had made good on its commitment. The product was named the XMC series, which stood for eXtreme Modulation Capacity. I immediately realized that XMC was short for Xi'an, Milan, and Chengdu, and it represented the joint innovation and development efforts of the three teams.

Commitment to Ambitious Goals Is the Best Motivation

Many challenges lay ahead as we tried to develop industry-leading microwave products. The design of super-high-frequency circuits for millimeter wave had long been recognized as a tough nut to crack. So we decided that for the E-band board, with a frequency of 80 GHz, it was important to have the R&D team and the manufacturing team in the same place. Standard practice was to have the two work relatively independently, but, on such a high-frequency board, even a tiny problem could have catastrophic consequences. We had to balance the possibility of problems during the design process against the need to maintain a reasonable profit margin. The team wanted to manufacture the board in China, but there were a number of technical difficulties, and we were having trouble importing some of the key components there. In the end, we all agreed that part of the 80 GHz board should be manufactured in Milan.

I found a consultant in Milan with extensive experience and expertise in manufacturing microwave products. With his help, the R&D team learned about the manufacturing process and key control points, which were critical to product quality assurance. We racked our brains for ways to increase the capacity of high-frequency system-in-a-package, and then shipped it back to our Chinese factory to be installed in the product.

Since we had never developed an E-band before, we spent a good few months doing tests and verification to solve problems.

Over the period, the E-band expert team worked day and night, tirelessly conducting experiments and solving problems. Once, a new problem occurred, causing a drop in our production capacity. So, a group of us travelled to our manufacturing facility in Song-shan Lake, where we worked with the teams from Xi'an, Chengdu, and Shanghai to identify the root cause. I still remember that trip to China, because I had broken my arm when I was playing basket-ball back home, and I had to wear a cast the whole time.

Much to our delight, we solved every problem. Now we have built a leading position in the microwave industry, and we now have the largest global market share.

Culture Is All About Adaptation

Over the past eight years, I have often been asked the same question: As a Westerner working for a Chinese company, how do you adapt to the different culture?

I don't think there is anything special. Though big companies have different management systems, they all share certain qualities. We just need to understand how to work in a big company.

Many non-Chinese managers at Huawei Europe have previously worked at the headquarters of big companies such as Ericsson and Siemens. They often come to me to seek advice on how to communicate with people at Huawei. I usually suggest that they should change their approach, because they haven't really understood that they are not in the company HQ any more (HQ is in China). No matter where you are, you need to adapt to the new company's values, the leaders, their way of working and their management style. You have to find how you can contribute.

You also need to learn about China and Huawei, and understand their culture and way of thinking, so as to better communicate with your colleagues. I first visited China 25 years ago, and travelled around many of the country's provinces. Wherever I went, I would take a tour, visit the scenic spots, and go to restaurants to try the local specialties. Gradually, I found myself falling in love with China, Chinese culture, and Chinese history.

I often tell the non-Chinese experts on my team to learn some basic Chinese, and not to always insist on eating Italian food, or going to fast food brands, or other Western restaurants. When you're in China, eat the food, because this is the way we can better understand our Chinese colleagues. Many of my Chinese colleagues ask me, "Can you speak Chinese?" I cannot actually speak the language, but I have learned about 300 to 400 Chinese characters. And those have been a very valuable tool for me.

Understanding a person is much more important than speaking a language. Charles Darwin explained that it is not the strongest who will survive, but those who adapt to a new environment quickly.

Culture is all about adapting and respecting diversity. No one expects me to behave exactly like a Chinese person. As an Italian, I respect Chinese culture and its people. Perhaps this is the reason why my Chinese colleagues so often choose to forgive and accept my mistakes.

Renato Lombardi and customers discuss the prototype built in Milan

Always Look on the Bright Side

How can we better adapt to a new environment? Personally speaking, I try to complain less and smile more, and always look on the bright side.

Eight years ago, Huawei was like a child, not yet in its teens. Though it was big, it was not mature in many ways. This was especially true of the processes and systems. Some colleagues used to complain a lot, and they would even ask me, "Renato, how come you never get angry?" I used to say, "We were hired to identify problems, propose suggestions, and solve the problems. All companies have problems as they grow and Huawei is no exception. If there were no problems, then why would we be here?"

I had a hard time fitting in here at first. But Huawei managers, especially senior executives, gave me a lot of support – in a way that I had never experienced before. Their support gave me confidence, and helped me find the best way to work with teams at HQ and across China.

I remember my first visit to Shenzhen after joining the company. I met senior executives, and they asked me, "How can we support you?" This was really impressive because, in most companies, you usually only meet senior executives to submit a report. Two hours after my meeting with the leadership, I started receiving calls from other colleagues who had been assigned to support me. I was deeply impressed by their leadership and ability to get things done. After that, every time I visited Shenzhen, I would send an email to various executives, and they would set aside some time to talk to me. At the end of each conversation, the executives would always ask, "How can I support you?"

A company cannot grow, improve, or change overnight. It takes time, and we need to be understanding. As long as we are heading in the right direction, we can be patient and wait for certain things to fall into place. It's like climbing a mountain. We may be attacked by mosquitoes along the way, but we shouldn't stop climbing. Our target is to climb to the top.

I trust my team; and I don't want to micromanage them. Everyone must take responsibility for their own work. If something needs to be done, you will do your utmost to get it done.

I'm a Wolf, Too

More than one Chinese colleague has said to me, "Renato, you are very Huawei." And I do think my character matches very well with Huawei's values.

During that period in Milan, I would arrive at the research lab early and leave late. After dinner with my family, I would turn on my laptop and continue working. That was my life, every day, regular as clockwork. I spent about 140 days travelling around the world every year, most often to China. Wherever I was, on the plane or the train, I would set up my laptop to work. I'm always thinking. As soon as I have an idea, I write it down. I love this job, and I have never drawn a distinction between my life and work, because work has always been a part of my life.

All the other microwave team members are similarly dedicated. There are now 50 people in the team. I don't check up on their work, because I trust my team; and I don't want to micromanage them. Everyone must take responsibility for their own work. If something needs to be done, you will do your utmost to get it done.

I like showing my staff card. I tell people, "My employee ID is 900004, which means I was the fourth non-Chinese employee in the European Research Institute, and the first one in the Microwave Division in Milan." It's a good reminder. I'm often the only non-Chinese employee present at meetings in China. I remember once, when we were discussing a confidential document, some of the people at the meeting didn't want to show it to me, because I wasn't Chinese. I showed them my Huawei ID card and said, "I work for this company, too. The moment I decided to work for Huawei, I made up my mind not to go halfway. But you may leave the company some day, so I have better reason to read that document than you." In the end, they showed me the document.

To this day, I still see myself as a lucky person. I'm lucky because I get to work with an excellent team, conduct industry-leading research, and contribute new thoughts and ideas. The Microwave Division in Milan started from nothing and has been growing ever since. It is like my baby, and it has become a part of me. Looking to the future, I see many opportunities awaiting us.

Someone once said to me that to work at Huawei you need to be aggressive like a wolf. So it's a good thing that I'm a wolf, too. I see both Italians and Chinese as pragmatists. No matter where you are from, as long as we can make the things everyone needs, the world will open its arms to us.

Renato Lombardi's lanyards from many technology conferences

Aesthetics: Adding a Human Touch to Technology

By Yin Yuanyuan

It was a sunny morning in September 2014. The Eiffel Tower loomed proudly nearby, flaunting its magnificence to the world. The golden dome of Les Invalides was shining in the sun, radiant with the stories of those who fought and died for the country.

The aroma of café au lait lingered on the sun-drenched balcony. Seated at a round table were three heavyweights from three very different fields: Ren Zhengfei, founder and CEO of Huawei; Cédric Villani, French mathematician and Fields medallist; and Mathieu Lehanneur, world-renowned designer. Their discussion ranged from mathematics and art, to philosophy and the future. Also present were engineers from Huawei's France Research Center and designers from Huawei's Aesthetics Research Center.

I was fortunate enough to be among them, sitting just an arm's length away, though the gap between me and the speakers felt enormous. Mr Ren has talked many times about "absorbing the energy of the cosmos over a cup of coffee". Well, here I was to witness it up close. After the meeting, Mr Ren asked us how the preparations for the Aesthetics Research Center were going, and encouraged us to be bolder and to experiment to find the right way forward.

That reminded me of the day in August 2013 when I was informed that I had been appointed director of the Aesthetics Research Center that was going to be stationed in Paris. It came as a surprise to me. I was delighted at the thought that I could go back to the country where I had studied and lived nine years earlier, yet that delight was soon followed by anxiety. The centre was to be Huawei's first facility dedicated to aesthetics design research. We had no examples to follow; we didn't even know yet in what areas we would work; and we had to decide for ourselves what the direction of our work would be and how we could translate what we were doing into business value. Amid these uncertainties, I went for my first meeting with the president of Huawei's 2012 Laboratories. His guidance and encouragement eased my worries and I started to have a clearer picture of what our goals were.

Location, Location, Location

The Aesthetics Research Center sits between three museums: the Louvre, the Musée d'Orsay, and the Musée Rodin. It overlooks Les Invalides and the Eiffel Tower, glories of the French nation.

Putting together a team and choosing a location were my initial priorities. I needed to find an office with an artistic touch. In the cold of November, I braved the drizzle and crisscrossed the city looking for potential locations. Back in my room at night, I was busy researching and planning. I decided to base our office

The balcony of the Aesthetics Research Center

The office at the Aesthetics Research Center

The reception area of the Aesthetics Research Center

in the 7th arrondissement, the political, cultural, and arts centre of Paris. After several rounds of talks with landlords, I narrowed my office options down to four.

In the end, we made our choice, HQ approved it, and 43 Rue Saint Dominique, Paris 75007 became the Huawei Aesthetics Research Center. We redesigned the office space to accommodate the needs of the centre. I was pushing to get the space ready for our designers so that they could begin to focus on their work. I came back to China, worked on the interior design plans during the day and negotiated prices with contractors in France over the phone in the evening. For once, the time difference was my ally. Within three months we had finished the fit-out, and moved into the new space in July 2014. Everyone was pleased with the simple and classic feel of our new workplace.

Setting Goals and Building a Team

Mr Ren once told the French media that France's expertise in colour could help us change the image of Huawei's products.

I believe that this expertise comes from the artistic culture. Art is abstract and all-encompassing and, for Parisians, anything – human or object – can be viewed through the lens of art. I was convinced that art was what Mr Ren was looking for when he decided to base the centre in Paris.

France is known around the world for its great painting, architecture, literature, and philosophy, and the country's artistry and craftsmanship have made it home to many of the world's top luxury brands. France is without a doubt the world's trendsetter in modern design. By feeling the pulse of design in Paris, and France as a whole, Huawei would be able to tap into and even shape consumer behaviour around the world. We all agreed that Paris was the right choice, and we were convinced that Huawei could benefit from being in this city – but what next? Our ideas were sketchy at best. What should we do?

"Let's steal a glance at the other side of the river: there seem to be cranes dancing gracefully," wrote Xu Chi in *Goldbach's Conjecture*. The way across the river is always filled with unknowns; you never know what the other side holds in store

The aesthetics team

for you until you get there. But amid uncertainty, the beauty of being human is that we can address each unknown one by one, turn them into knowns, and build a bridge to the other side. How could we build that bridge for the Aesthetics Research Center?

First, we needed a professional team. After more than a year of recruitment efforts, we had put together our design team in Paris. Our team had colour and material designers and brand designers from the auto industry; a visual communication designer from Le Bon Marché; a watch designer from Dior; a digital visual design specialist from Chanel; and a jewellery designer from Boucheron. After eight months of talks and negotiation, we also managed to persuade Mathieu Lehanneur, a world-renowned design genius, to join the team as chief designer. He is known for integrating innovations in design, science, technology, and art into his intensely user-oriented creations. This philosophy is very much at one with Huawei's.

It was an excellent team, and we often had productive brainstorming sessions during the project development period. We created various mood boards and were able to contribute opinions on design from the perspective of different domains. By throwing ideas back and forth, the aesthetics team worked hard to define a new style for Huawei.

What should the Huawei style look like? This was one of the challenging problems we faced.

First, 'new Huawei' should be elegant and simple, because simplicity is the future. Second, materials. We had to use natural and real materials, and exquisite craftwork to reflect the high quality of Huawei products and the company's spirit of craftsmanship. Real crafted products and tailored services can build our customers' trust in Huawei. Third, a new interpretation of 'Huawei red'. The red Huawei logo represents Huawei's 29 years of dedication. During that period, 180,000 Huawei employees have worked hard together, but now Huawei is entering uncharted territory. Can we convey 'new Huawei' more confidently and elegantly? Does the Huawei logo have to be red? Can we find a more subtle way

Technology is powerful, but people don't care about technology per se. Instead, they focus on how technology can improve their lives.

to show the red logo, for example, by using different lamplight effects or with translucent materials?

Huawei is a high-tech company. Technology is powerful, but people don't care about technology per se. Instead, they focus on how technology can improve their lives. So, if we want to win customers with technology, we must turn it into something customers really want. We need to embed technology into our designs to serve customers and create value. In other words, we need to convey our image and philosophy in a more human way, so that customers can feel for themselves that Huawei is putting them at the centre of everything we do. That is a much better feeling than cold technology.

We are living in an era of digital interaction and we are standing at a new turning point in history. Following the industrial revolution of the 19th century and the digital revolution of the 20th century, we are entering a new era of interpersonal relations – digital technology has completely changed the way we interact with others. Now, we need to adopt new approaches to improve customers' experience as they interact with Huawei.

Our team decided to apply the new visual identity (VI) series across Huawei's products, expo displays, external communications, and the design of our exhibition halls and flagship stores. We wanted to create a more open and progressive company image through Huawei's products and spaces, so that customers could feel the spirit of Huawei without even seeing our logo. Huawei wants to convey much more than technology. We are connecting people and providing them with the best experience – and this enables us to get closer to our customers.

This new style concept, the new VI, made us very excited. Once most of the leadership team had understood and approved what we were doing, our team started to focus on this project.

Agnès Larnicol was the first local staff member to join the team. Our office in Paris was not yet ready, so I invited her to come to Shenzhen with me and work on the colour, material, and finish (CMF) design for devices. She had never worked on

CMF for consumer electronics before, but with her feel for colour, she produced an amazing solution. Two months after she joined our team, Apple launched its first Apple Watch. I found that the four-colour scheme in Agnès's original design for Huawei wristband wearables was identical to the scheme used for the Apple Watch. The whole team was very excited about this. Mr Ren had specifically asked us to research colour in Paris, and this coincidence boosted our confidence. Later, many projects demonstrated that our team was able to predict which colours and styles would be in fashion and be accepted by consumers.

Based on our newly-defined Huawei style, our team delivered multiple projects, and we started to get a sense for our role and position in the company. We focused our skills and goals on studying the latest design trends, on innovative design, and brand design. We realized that our team should regularly produce trend reports to guide Huawei product design globally. We needed to integrate France's experience in the luxury and watch industries into the innovation process, integrate design and VI into our corporate identity, and incorporate aesthetics into our brand. We knew we could raise the quality of Huawei's brand image. After more than a year's hard work, we gradually developed a picture of the ultimate goal.

First Try at The Mobile World Congress

"The Aesthetics Research Center is Huawei's smallest research division. I am confident that it will soon become an important part of Huawei's global innovation – not just in France, but also around the world. By combining aesthetics with technology, we will be able to give 'cold' technology a 'warm' human touch," rotating CEO Ken Hu said at the opening ceremony in Paris on 12 March 2015.

I often asked myself, in a technology company like Huawei, where does the aesthetics team fit in? How do we identify ourselves? How far can we go? Ken Hu's speech inspired every team member, and we realized that our mission is to add warmth to Huawei.

The opening of the Aesthetics Research Center

Later, Mathieu Lehanneur and I gave a 30-minute report to the executive management team. At that meeting, Mr Ren remarked, "Your responsibility is to change Huawei's corporate image. The Mobile World Congress (MWC) 2016 will be your first outing. Make the Huawei booth the brightest star in Barcelona!" Let a team less than two years old take charge of designing the Huawei booth for the MWC? I suddenly felt that the pressure was on.

I met Jacques Séguéla for coffee in Shanghai, bathed in the neon lights of the Oriental Pearl Tower. As a leading creative figure in Europe, he successfully promoted many famous brands worldwide, such as Citroen, Evian, Louis Vuitton, Dior, and Air France. In order to prepare for the design of the Huawei booth at the MWC, I asked him what he thought Huawei should look like. His reply was: "Elegant, fluent, and human, with an oriental flavour." Séguéla believed that following Europe and the US would get us nowhere, and Huawei should demonstrate its own cultural identity.

Living in a fast-changing era, we can only go far if we look far ahead. The key to our corporate image is whether the consumers of a certain market can relate to the image. We felt the next step was to present our cultural identity on a global stage. We had to make creativity a new driving force behind the company's development, build a new corporate image, and find new ways to present it.

As we prepared for the MWC, we tried to experiment with Huawei's technology, and to discover a more modern, human, nimble, and refined way to interpret Huawei's future. Gradually the design came together. The sky represented the boundless connected world, with a white Huawei logo in the sky to convey harmony and inclusiveness. The oriental elegance of the design instantly resonated with customers. The lines of the logo were extended into six taut curves, conveying the power and impact of a more confident Huawei. These six lines flowed confidently through the words 'A Better Connected World'. Three red arrows under the white Huawei logo represented the efforts of Huawei's

Preparing for the MWC

180,000 employees, who have worked with passion to make the company an industry leader. At the MWC, the aesthetics team proposed this brand new visual design for Huawei, and further defined the company's tone of voice, image, and design language to enhance customers' awareness.

The MWC project team invited two well-known international design companies to compete with our aesthetics team. After many rounds of presentations and selections, our designs won the approval of all our internal stakeholders. The corporate leadership asked us to think about how to build up Huawei's image as a more open and collaborative company, aiming to achieve win–win results in our future work.

The entrance to our 67m-wide booth was 27m wide. Visitors appeared to be walking under a blue sky as they approached the entrance. The glass floor, and the 11 ticket barriers and benches made of polished metal, all reflected the light of the sky. Sitting on the benches, visitors were immersed in an amazing digital world created by Huawei. The large entrance was also a place for visitors to rest, share ideas, and engage with each other. It was an open entryway to digital blue skies.

Huawei's booth at the MWC 2016

Huawei's booth at the MWC 2016

A long passageway ran down the centre of the booth, connecting the whole space, with white displays resembling islets
under the blue dome. Our booth presented visitors a harmoni-
ous picture of Huawei working with its partners in pursuit of
shared success. Walking down the passageway, visitors were led
into the future world, made vivid and realistic by Huawei (with
its data pipes) in cooperation with its partners.

On the second floor, the meeting room and the relaxation area
took up a huge open space. Tucked behind the meeting room was
a charming balcony with wooden railings, with the best view
of the 'Open ROADS' central passageway. Floating above the
centre was the immense ceiling screen, with images of blue sky
and white fluffy clouds, orienting our visitors on their journey
through the digital world. We were able to project a brand new
image of Huawei to our visitors by sharing and engaging with
them in this space of data pipes, harmony, and shared success.

Of course, a lot of effort went on behind the scenes. Brainstorming sessions in Shanghai, original designs and prototypes
in Paris, and then presentations and approvals: the whole process took eight months. During that time, we developed and

The Huawei booth used to be somewhat mysterious. This year, it was open and inviting, showcasing a more confident and inclusive Huawei.

improved the design repeatedly. We had to ensure consistency across multiple channels, including visual communication, video, and print. We thus had to draw up detailed guidelines, specifying everything from the colours and materials to be used in the furniture and lamps, and how they should go together, to the uniforms and painting of the booth. We inspected the colours and the quality of the painting work personally, and spent three weeks in Barcelona setting up our booth. The designers committed to the challenge with utter dedication. They shuttled between cities, working long hours, sometimes to 2am in the morning. They braved pouring rain, worksite dust, and endless noise over the three weeks of construction. Their meticulous attention to detail enabled us to present Huawei as an open, inclusive leader.

One customer told me that he had been visiting the Huawei booth at MWC for ten years and he had seen little change in all that time. This year, however, he saw something very different. The Huawei booth used to be somewhat mysterious. This year, it was open and inviting, showcasing a more confident and inclusive Huawei.

The Taste of Success

After the MWC, the aesthetics team sat together in a Catalonia coffee shop. The Spanish coffee was as strong as ever, yet slightly different this time. Our months of hard work had been as bitter as coffee beans, but the invigorating feedback we got from our customers lingered on like the aroma of a fresh roast. We talked about Catalonian art and debated the new VI and new ways to express Huawei. We absorbed the energy of the design world over those cups of coffee, flinging ideas back and forth like the fabled debaters of Athens.

From Challenger to Champion

By Chuan Cheng

On 4 March 2015, amid the clicking of camera shutters, the president of Huawei Products & Solutions, Ryan Ding, made his way onto the stage during the Mobile World Congress (MWC), the world's largest gathering for the mobile industry. He was about to receive the Best Mobile Infrastructure Award from the president of GSMA on behalf of Huawei.

"This award commends Huawei for its use of small cell technology to help telecom operators improve indoor mobile broadband coverage, quality, and capacity, in a CAPEX-friendly manner." The award introduction was announced to thunderous applause. Under the brilliant stage lights, the Huawei logo glimmered on the massive screen.

The term 'small cell', formerly not well known, has begun to appear frequently in various award lists, and global market demand is increasing rapidly. Despite various uncertainties over the past decade, we have been fortunate enough to have had opportunities to develop this fascinating technology.

The Emergence of a Wireless 'Challenge Team'

When I graduated in 2005, I was full of hope and dreams. My first job in wireless communications was as a software engineer at Huawei. At that time, Huawei's 2G products were mainstream, and 3G was still in an exploratory phase. However, there were already experts predicting explosive growth in mobile user data volume. A new wireless communications base station, known as Femto, applied in indoor environments such as households and offices, was increasingly being talked about.

Femto was easy to instal and could be placed anywhere with signal access to rapidly augment the signal strength. Telecom operators were very enthusiastic about the product, and many consulting companies predicted that the 'Femto Era' had arrived. They estimated that, by 2010, global annual shipping volume could reach into the millions of units.

Ryan Ding receiving the award at the MWC

In the traditional telecom industry, wireless networks were primarily deployed using macro base stations. However, these presented major technical barriers, and only large vendors were able to manufacture them. With the advent of Femto, a glimmer of hope was seen by IT vendors itching to get a piece of the action in the communications industry. At the same time, chip manufacturers were also clamouring to release chip series. The aim was to make the development of wireless base stations as easy as wifi and to greatly reduce the threshold for market access.

Suddenly, I found more than 100 enterprises around me capable of focusing on wireless small cells. Many of my former classmates were joining small base station companies no one had ever heard of. In order to survive, these small companies routinely engaged in price battles, and there was a dazzling array of offerings available. This severely affected the quality of network solutions. Low quality and low prices contradicted the demands for high reliability and high stability.

In the middle of all of this, the senior management of Huawei's Wireless Network Product Line made a cautious but innovative decision: it would establish a 'Challenge Team' in the wireless division focused on the end-to-end Femto solution. The so-called

Challenge Team was a group specifically tasked with playing the part of the competition and aiming to 'challenge' our solutions. The team members would play the role of a competitor and carry out targeted training of our 'Principal Forces'. There were two goals to having a Challenge Team in the wireless business. The first was to play the part of our competitor IT vendors and to constantly challenge the traditional product teams, forcing us to beef up our capabilities. The second goal was to face up against IT vendors through exceptional network performance backed up by the company's robust solutions and technology.

One day in late 2007, I was deep in thought considering the difficulties of delivery when my manager called me into a meeting room and gave me a choice. He said: "The product line will be putting together a Femto R&D team. They want you to be the project leader for one of the groups. Are you up for that?" Feeling quite confident, I accepted without any reservations and followed in the footsteps of over 60 other Femto team members to the Chengdu Research Center.

An oath-taking ceremony for the Femto team's relocation to
the Chengdu Research Center in July 2008

Welcoming us was a one-storey office building in the Incubation Park. Above the elevator was a red banner, which read: "We started in Shanghai and will shine in Chengdu." Today, whenever I visit the Chengdu Research Center on business and see the small cell products lined up in the dedicated U1 exhibition hall, I always think back to that red banner.

Experiencing the Early Demise of Femto

It was in 2008 that China deployed 3G networks on a large scale. It was also the year that I started to use my first large-screen smartphone. However, indoors, the phone would regularly only have 2G signals, and it was infuriatingly slow to open a web page. In order to quickly ramp up indoor network quality, one Chinese telecom operator turned its sights to new base stations, such as Femto. Based on its confidence in Huawei built over many years, the telecom operator made a request to purchase 1 million Femto units and specifically selected 17 May 2009 (International Telecommunications Day) as the official start of commercial usage.

Not a few thousand, not tens of thousands – a million units. I had long since heard about the difficulties faced by the company's GSM and UMTS in the early days. And yet here was our team, which had received this enormous order just after a year. Unsurprisingly, we novices were so excited about the opportunity that we could hardly sleep. When our manager rushed into the lab to tell us this exciting news, the entire team went crazy with joy. That evening, we went to have a meal of hot pot. Scarlet red hot peppers bubbled and popped in the broiling pot. We drank and were merry, speaking loudly, our hearts full of dreams of a wonderful future.

The next day, the Femto Development Department organized a staff-wide mobilization meeting. At the meeting, you would have heard us repeating grandiose phrases, such as: "Today we've got an order for a million units, and tomorrow we're going to bring Femto to every residential area."

Everything started with chips. This was the secret of the wireless base station's success. We unequivocally chose to stand upon the shoulders of giants and to make a dedicated chip of our own. However, as we delved deeper into the process of development, various issues arose. We began to experience scope creep in the project, and a sense of worry sprouted and spread within the team. May 17 was no longer the date on which we expected victory, but instead seemed to us like an impending disaster, our very own Sword of Damocles suspended above our head.

In order to ensure the sample chip could be received prior to 1 January 2009, we specially assigned a project leader to pick up the chip from Hong Kong and return it to the Chengdu Research Center. Our manager held another internal mobilization meeting, and organized a special action team. The original plan of ten months from receiving the chip to delivery was abruptly shrunk down to five months – and we delivered Huawei's first Femto base station on time.

This was the first commercial product that I had been responsible for developing. When I first laid eyes on it, it was like seeing my newborn child. The air around me seemed to condense, and I took the dainty box in my hand and softly caressed it, fearful of doing it any harm. This product won us many honours. It was the first wireless product to receive the Red Dot Award. It was the first product to be put into commercial use on a public network and also the first household plug-and-play product.

Just as we were about to celebrate, though, we received the terrible news that our customer was cancelling the order. Our manager tried to emphasize that it wasn't that we hadn't done a good job. Rather, it was because the strategy for network construction of the telecom operator had changed. But I couldn't hear a word of it. My mind was running in a loop over and over, replaying the countless days and nights we had spent in development. My colleagues were in the same frame of mind as I was, and we all quietly continued with our work in the lab, amid the stifling atmosphere.

Over the next three years, at the same time as continuing to optimize our products, each day we waited for the market to emerge. Within China and abroad there were over 20 telecom operator networks being put into commercial use, some with several thousand units as small-scale trials, and some with just dozens being used as experimental deployments. We were seeing a lot of hope, but also experiencing a lot of disappointment. The ambition to ship a million units was slipping through our fingers. The dream of bringing Femto to every residential area was fading further and further from view.

Ultimately, telecom operators also gradually gave up on this idea. Our total shipped volume over four years was less than 100,000 units. The department headcount shrank from its heyday number of 140 people down to just 70.

Were we really just going to give up on it?

If You Want to Live, Then You've Got to Find New Life

In 2012, the Femto field, led by chip manufacturers like Qualcomm and Broadcom, saw the rise of a new player, which I'll call 'Corporation C'. Corporation C proposed the strategy of 'Inside-Out' during that year's MWC. They stated that they would absorb all traffic from indoor small cells and completely upend traditional macro cell networks. The entire wifi long cellular solution could turn a deployed wifi access point into a wireless base station through a simple modification.

Corporation C leveraged its channel advantages to explore a new business model. This model focused on selling wireless cellular equipment to enterprise owners through channel partners, which could then be reverse-leased to telecom operators as a way to share profits. If this happened, then traffic would no longer be passing through the wide pipes we had built with telecom operators over many years, but instead would see outdoor macro cell networks likely play a supporting role. I was floored by this innovation.

Discussions were heated, but the strategic window of opportunity was closing, and we had to act quickly if we were going to seize it.

It was then that I realized that we, the Challenge Team, had kept our heads down to the exclusion of all else and had mistakenly only focused on making boxes. We had failed to learn about the overall solutions and market information relating to small cells. We had failed to give consideration to the network as a whole. This meant that our solutions were definitely not going to be an attractive option to telecom operators. Therefore, I decided to work in the Product Management Department to gain better insight into the market. I wanted an end-to-end view of products, so that we could put together the most competitive solutions possible.

My new work involved getting R&D system engineers at various levels together for discussions and to systematically gain an understanding of our business model. At the time, the most prominent means of achieving indoor coverage was an indoor distributed antenna system – the 'mushroom antenna' often seen in shopping malls and office buildings. This type of system only provided voice and low-speed data service, and it wasn't able to meet the growing demand for high-speed data service.

Each expert proposed various competitive ideas that could basically be broken down into three camps: 1) The 'Radical Camp' wanted to use small cells to entirely replace the 'mushroom antennas' and to capture the traditional indoor distributed network market; 2) The 'Moderate Camp' suggested making improvements to the 'mushroom antennas' and sharing the market with other solutions. This would save on investment costs while also ensuring some profits were realized; 3) The 'Conservative Camp' was of the opinion that the indoor distributed market was subject to significant non-technical influences and that the hurdles were more in discussing site selection with building owners. They suggested using existing macro cell solutions, leveraging outdoor resources as a strategy to accelerate indoor market development.

Discussions were heated, but the strategic window of opportunity was closing, and we had to act quickly if we were going to seize it. In order to wrap up discussions as quickly as possible, our team organized multiple closed-door workshops and internal competitions between teams. Ultimately, everyone agreed to use LampSite, an indoor distributed digital cellular system, to tackle the indoor coverage market. The name LampSite was chosen because we hoped that our indoor wireless base stations could be as simple to instal as a light bulb, and that they would illuminate each building just like lamps.

If you want to live, then you have to find new purpose. So we enthusiastically delved into our second major endeavour.

A 'Difficult to Leave' Lecture Stand

Bringing the condensed wisdom of the group with me, I confidently took to the stage of the Integrated Project Management Team (IPMT) meeting to report on the project initiation. I never imagined what I would face.

I encountered the most aggressive questioning of my professional career on two occasions at IPMT meetings. In the face of the challenges from the committee members, I was only just able to scrape by with my dignity intact. The sweat was pouring off my forehead, and soon my clothing was drenched. The air in the room seemed to have coalesced, making it impossible to breath. Even though the entire solution had already been cut at the knees, I still wasn't able to squeeze out a 'pass'. My mind was a blank as I left the meeting room. I really didn't have it in me to continue.

After one of the meetings, my manager drove me home. The sunlight that day was blinding, and there was a strong wind blowing. My manager saw how discouraged I was. He said calmly: "The small cell is a wireless product that is most closely related to IT, and it is also the most innovative. It's never going to be smooth sailing when you're trying to innovate. The questioning of the others was because they felt it was the only way to find the best way forward." I knew that, because of our previous experience, the wireless product line was more cautious in its decision-making for this all-new LampSite solution. We just had to clear up their doubts. I had a special place in my heart for this product on which I had spent five years of my life. I didn't want to give up.

Moving forward, we synchronized our efforts with the field technical sales teams in the service product line, the China Region, Southeast Asia, and South Pacific. We engaged in more in-depth diagnostic testing and gained better insight into the market space and how the industry chain worked. Not only did we have to ensure our technology was competitive, but we also had to prove that the business model for LampSite was feasible.

This time, we prepared 100 pages of materials, including everything from market space insights, to an analysis of technological competition, the strategic steps of delivery, and marketing strategy. We provided detailed responses to the outstanding issues raised by the IPMT committee members. In addition to this, we boldly proposed integrating industry resources to create an industry platform, which would allow further sharing of benefits.

Ultimately, I finally received the result I was hoping for – the project was approved. I still remember very clearly that, after the meeting, my manager sent an email to our team saying, "Good on you guys!"

The Pickiest Customer Said: "The First Bite Was Delicious!"

Even though the project was approved, we didn't receive support to move the project towards commercial rollout. Even with the best idea, all we really had was useless diagrams and schematics. We didn't have a telecom operator lined up as the first adopter. What could we do?

I decided to drag along a couple of R&D colleagues on a trip to Japan, the most developed mobile broadband market, to look for opportunities. In Japan at the time, major hubs of data traffic, like Ginza Tokyo, were seeing explosive growth. Traditional solutions were simply not able to satisfy market demand.

Then Wireless Network Product Line President, Wang Tao, recommended LampSite to the CTO of a tier-1 telecom operator in Japan. The product was an instant hit: The customer loved it and kept repeating to himself, "This is exactly what I want." He enthusiastically started going over the details with his technical team. Upon hearing him say this, one of Huawei's translators passed the exciting news on to field technical sales colleagues. As expected, several days later the field office received a formal letter from the customer asking Huawei to provide a complete commercial solution as quickly as possible. They even promised to pay for R&D expenses up front.

At such a critical juncture, the customer gave us the opportunity that we needed. Wang Tao said earnestly: "You have to help the customer truly address the issue of high traffic indoors." The countdown was on once again. This was different from the last endeavour. We didn't have the shoulders of giants upon which to stand. We all had to become giants ourselves.

Through multiple visits to key customers, we gained insight into their requirements for indoor coverage solutions. We discovered that the biggest issues for telecom operators in traditional indoor distributed systems were capacity restrictions and deployment challenges. They wanted to greatly improve capacity while being able to quickly deploy the solution.

To achieve this, we put our minds to work thinking again about every detail of the solution. We incorporated the advantages of IT systems into wireless cellular technology. The most typical application was our use of regular network cables to solve the issue of power supply and transmission for remote radio frequency (RF) units. This involved some of our independently developed key technologies – CPRI OVER network cable, CPRI signal compression, and high power network cable power supplies. These technologies helped the indoor cellular systems of telecom operators evolve beyond cumbersome RF feeder and power cables. It was possible to provide indoor mobile broadband coverage by using just one normal network cable.

I had long since heard about how strict Japanese customers were regarding product quality. But I never imagined that the customer would measure the length, width, and height of the modules themselves, or that they would calculate the product volume and weight. Their measurements were precise down to two decimal places, and they even tested each of several dozen metrics for our filters. A small air bubble on the surface coating would be reason enough to have the product marked as non-compliant.

During the Chinese Spring Festival of 2013, intermediate RF and base station platform colleagues spent some time at the Songshan Lake production line in Guangdong, China. They went there to learn about customer requirements placed on other product lines and also to continually improve their own product offerings and processing. In order to remain on schedule, many staff worked on the production line on 12-hour shifts for a month and carried out thermal stress screening on every single product. These efforts ultimately enabled them to ship out over 300 modules of high quality.

Wireless Network Product Line President Wang Tao
unveiling LampSite at the MWC

In June 2013, the first generation of LampSite products was officially released and sent to the global market. The customer received the product on time and as expected. I could sense the ice finally thawing in our business. Soon after, the network experience offered by LampSite caught the attention of customers in regions including China, the South Pacific, Southeast Asia, and Europe. The solution was installed at locations such as Beijing Capital Airport, the Great Hall of the People, the Evian Royal Hotel in France, and the Royal Opera House in Spain.

For us youthful fellows who had 'grown up' as a result of experiencing the Femto fiasco, the success came a bit too quickly. This time around, though, we really did see the light of victory.

The first generation of LampSite only marked the start of the race for us.

During the course of developing the second generation of products, hardware engineers innovated by applying device 'frequency selection' technology into LampSite. No matter which telecom operator used the solution, the product allowed for automatic selection of appropriate technical standards and frequency. This was similar to mobile phone users not needing to know whether they are using LTE or UMTS in order to enjoy high-speed networks. Telecom operators no longer had to worry about future new spectrum that would have previously necessitated a hardware upgrade. Antenna engineers were also able to further reduce the size of the product and integrated a dozen antennas onto a space the size of two palms. Installation engineers spent four years researching the invention of an installation method allowing the installer to simply push and lock the unit into place in just ten seconds. The structural design team reduced the ceiling space occupied by LampSite from 30mm down to 20mm, and then down to 10mm, achieving a more aesthetically pleasing integration of the attractive small white box with its environment.

The LampSite pioneer team at the Songshan Lake Production Line
on 1 January 2013

All Players Became Allies

Apart from the technical solutions, the most difficult challenge
facing telecom operators in relation to indoor coverage was
space in buildings. This was because traditional solutions could
generate revenue from lease fees, making them less than willing
to make the switch to the new system. To address this issue,
Small Cell Product Line President, Zhou Yuefeng, guided the
team in thinking about the foundational business model. This
ultimately led to the concept of site crowdsourcing. Similar to
crowdsourcing for internet innovation, site crowdsourcing
allowed telecom operators, sites, enterprises, telecom equipment suppliers, internet enterprises, and developers to explore
new ways of collaborating from the very beginning right up to
final operation.

For example, we found that a lot of popular navigational software became unusable indoors because there was no GPS signal. We seized on this opportunity to proactively contact electronic map providers. By linking the network up with their servers, users could continue to seamlessly use navigational services even when indoors. Another example is that currently our cell phones show our signal as being 'China Mobile 4G', or 'China Unicom 4G' and so on. Moving forward, we could begin to see things like 'China Mobile – Starbucks 4G', and China Mobile users would be able to enjoy free data traffic, free calling, and other special deals.

In 2015 and 2016, we established national industry alliances involving small cells in countries including Indonesia, Malaysia, and the Philippines. Part of the aim of doing so has been to help the idea of site crowdsourcing take root locally. A telecom operator in Canada swapped shares with a power company to instal large quantities of small cells on the latter's power poles and other infrastructure. Another telecom operator cooperated with a Dutch bus stop ad company, using the space around bus stops to instal small cells. The advertising company was able to receive lease income while also leveraging the telecom operator's big data capabilities to dynamically and precisely place advertising. All players along the industry chain in this region saw their fates become intertwined and they began to collaboratively promote the development of indoor mobile broadband.

At the same time, other small cell products emerged alongside LampSite and opened up the market space even further. This brought customers a truly phenomenal network experience.

What's Next?

A decade ago we were talking about small cells, and there was a lot of uncertainty. Today we are still talking about small cells, and there is still a lot of uncertainty. But, within all of this uncertainty, there is one thing that is certain, and that is that finding a direction that truly aligns with the development requirements of telecom operators is of utmost importance.

From a challenger to a champion and back again. The industry is in a constant state of flux and self-renewal. A decade is a long time in one's professional career. I have been lucky enough to see the birth of a new product and its eventual take-off and flight to higher heights.

Huawei held a small cell industry alliance preparation summit in collaboration with multiple Malaysian telecom operators and site owners

Riding the Microwave to Success

By Zhang Jichao

I was 28 years old in 2005, which was my fifth year at Huawei. One day, a manager said to me, "We have decided to develop microwave products. Would you like to join us?" Though I wasn't all that familiar with the field of microwaves, I still decided to join them. In fact, nobody on our team knew much about microwave technology, which was perhaps an indication of some overconfidence.

To Take a Short Cut or Develop Our Own Microwave Products?

The Chinese New Year was approaching. A team member asked me if we had to work during the holiday. After some thought, I told him that we didn't have to work, but everyone would be receiving a book: *Digital Microwave Communication Technology*. This was a Chinese New Year gift and our task was to read through the book during the seven-day holiday. I told everyone that we would be tested on it after getting back to work. This nearly 500-page book was a tough read and full of technical terms. It was a real challenge for us to finish it in just a week. As I read through it, I found that the knowledge I had previously acquired on communication engineering and digital signal processing in university was quite useful. I also wished I had paid more attention to the two subjects at the time. Anyway, we studied hard during the holiday and devoted ourselves to a month of workshops on microwave technology as soon as we returned. Through these efforts, we gained a general understanding of microwaves.

At the beginning, we assumed it would be easy to produce microwave equipment. Our first method involved combining an intermediate frequency (IF) board with a mature optical transmission product. However, further analysis of this method revealed that such products would not be competitive in terms of bandwidth, performance, and cost. We then looked at a second method, but challenging technical problems remained, such as the layout of architecture, heat dissipation, and power consumption.

Our team members were deeply divided about which of the two methods to choose. Some advocated the first approach, as they thought it would allow us to launch the product quickly. Others thought we should produce our own competitive and unique microwave equipment, and build Huawei's own brand in the market.

We held a meeting at the Ming Wah International Convention Center in Shenzhen and invited managers and experts involved in transmission technology to join our discussion. Microwave equipment was sparsely deployed across a tiny bandwidth, and there were no systems available to centrally manage the highly dispersed equipment. So, it was difficult to determine where equipment was installed and how well it operated. This meant we were unable to rapidly identify and tackle any issues that might arise. After an animated discussion, we arrived at a conclusion that was important for the development of microwave technology. We would increase the bandwidth while developing networked microwave equipment that could be centrally managed and maintained. This would allow us to track the operation of the equipment in real time, no matter where it was installed.

This meeting became a milestone in the history of microwave development. After our discussion, we invited more than a dozen top experts – in fields such as system integration, architecture, and heat dissipation – to join us for a one-month-long project in Chengdu focused on research into networked microwave equipment. We first solved the problem of building a new architecture. Owing to our lack of knowledge about analog IF technology, we also invited Peter Zhao, an expert from the company's wireless department, and other well-known microwave experts from around the country to join us in building a new system architecture.

However, we soon encountered another problem. Because we did not have our own chips, radio frequency modules, antennas, or other components, we were unable to manufacture the microwave products ourselves. We therefore had to seek outside partners. This was no easy feat. We contacted almost every microwave supplier in the market, but they all doubted our ability to develop microwave products. After hearing the concerns of so many microwave suppliers, I also started to doubt if we could develop microwave products. But we had no choice but to struggle on and find a solution.

We ultimately found several good suppliers with whom we could cooperate. We launched our first microwave product – the OptiX RTN 600 – in 2006, based on our design of system architecture, expertise in IF technology, and competitive edge in optical technology and networks.

First Cooperation with a Top Operator

As IP networks became dominant in 2007, microwave was once again in vogue. Ryan Ding, the president of Huawei's Network Product Line at the time, took us on a visit to Vodafone. We identified an opportunity to cooperate with Vodafone on the IP microwave solution. After the meeting, Vodafone took the initiative to invite a public tender. This was the first time we were bidding to work with a major operator, so we attached great importance to this opportunity.

In September, we travelled to Milan, Italy – the birthplace of microwave technology – to participate in a bid clarification meeting with Vodafone. During the meeting, we were interrupted many times and a technical expert at Vodafone even directly rebuked us, saying, "You don't fully understand our network architecture. Your solution is not competitive and just looks like sloppy work." It was tough to hear these words.

Nonetheless, Vodafone was still interested in our concept of networked microwave design and we were given another opportunity for bid clarification in a month. We knew that this might be our last chance. We basically lived at the Milan office during that time. In the mornings, we would work with our employees in Milan to analyse and deepen our understanding of the bidding documents and go over key points. In the afternoons and evenings we would discuss the customer's questions with our

R&D team in China. The following morning we would write out a detailed answer to every question from Vodafone and get the answers translated into English.

A month later, we met with our customer once again. After I completed the bid clarification on behalf of our team, the Vodafone representative who had criticized us at the last meeting said to us, "It is amazing that you have made such great progress within such a short period of time." During our third bid clarification meeting with Vodafone, we invited experts from our European Research Center to explain our solution in greater depth. After listening to the explanations, it was clear that we had won over the representative who had previously been unsatisfied. She smiled and said, "It looks like you can offer exactly what we want. I'm satisfied with your solution this time." Through two rounds of clarification, we earned the customer's trust and recognition, and were able to form our own concept to develop microwave equipment.

This was our first time participating in bid clarification meetings with one of the leading operators in the industry. Although the process was hard, the meetings enabled us to accurately understand the market requirements for microwave equipment as networks transitioned towards IP, and helped Huawei take early steps in this transformation to build influence in the microwave industry. There was a joyful, tear-filled scene when we told our team members back in China that we had won the bid.

Product Development and Admission Test

We did not have much time to revel in the success, however, as we had to get down to work on product R&D immediately. Vodafone required that our products pass the admission test within seven months, though the product development normally took ten months. Also, this was the first time we'd had to apply a key chip, so it was even more challenging. At the kick-off meeting, our managers reiterated multiple times this was going to be a 'mission impossible', but they admitted there was no other choice. We simply had to finish the product development within seven months. In order to speed up the process, our team members often worked overtime, slept in the office, and would often even forego a morning shave.

In May 2008, we reached the most difficult R&D stage and had to skip the May Day holiday. We wrote code, set up test environments, discussed solutions, and prepared to test the board. By 7 May, we were testing the board in the lab, but found something wrong with the 85X2 chip. In order to troubleshoot the problem, we stayed up late testing the board over and over again. Despite our best efforts, we failed to determine the exact problem and couldn't get the system up and running. We were getting anxious as we looked at the calendar and thought about how much work still remained before the hard deadline. So we decided to establish a special team to troubleshoot the 85X2 chip. We invited hardware, software, and chip experts to join us, aiming to get the system fully operational as quickly as possible.

Team members in the lab working on the solution for Vodafone's admission test

That day, every team member was focused on testing the 85X2 chip, but the issue still hadn't been uncovered by the evening. We were running out of time and everyone was anxious, deciding to forego dinner in favour of spending extra time on the issue at hand. We, once again, gathered the team together and brainstormed solutions to the chip issue.

At 11 o'clock that night, one of our team members came up with an idea that could possibly help identify the problem. A glimmer of hope shone across our faces, and we quickly got down to examining the design and software configuration again, reviewing and rewriting code, and re-loading it onto the board. Finally, we tested the board again – and the system began to work.

"It's connected! It's connected! The system is working!" We were so excited we erupted into cheers and laughter in the lab.

Winning Over a Tough Customer

Vodafone decided to test our product on the eve of the Chinese New Year. Without hesitation, our team members chose to stay behind to work rather than head home to celebrate the holiday with their loved ones. Due to the time difference between China and Europe, we adjusted our work schedule based on the customer's needs. From 3pm to 9pm Beijing time, we worked with the customer to test our product. Then, and from 9pm to 3pm Beijing time, while the customer was not working, we burned through the night to identify and resolve problems that the customer had presented during the testing process, rewriting code, and retesting the updated version.

Vodafone was very strict about this process. Before the testing started, they asked us to finalize the versions of software and hardware that were subject to the testing and they would not allow us to change versions during the process. When a problem arose, we had to locate it and clearly explain the cause. When testing the reliability of the board, Vodafone would reseat the board hundreds of times a day. Every time a problem occurred, Vodafone halted the testing and asked us to give an explanation.

Whenever the customer was testing our microwave products, all members of the team remained in the office in the event of any urgent needs.

We worked into the early hours of the first day of the Chinese New Year. Just when we were about to hit the hay, we received a call and heard that a problem had occurred during the board reseating test. A group of team members plunged into this issue and were finally able to locate the problem. We got down to work analysing the cause, modified the version, and sent the update to our testing team members who were working with Vodafone on-site.

Whenever the customer was testing our microwave products, all members of the team remained in the office in the event of any urgent needs. When we were sleepy, we would walk around the office or play a round of table tennis in the corridor. And when we were hungry, we cooked up a pack of instant noodles. Two weeks later, we finally received the test report from the customer, which came with the note, "It's amazing that you were able to make it. We are satisfied with the great test results."

In the movie series *Mission Impossible*, Ethan Hunt always has advanced weapons and fast cars at his disposal when tasked with a tough assignment. He could also leap from the ground to a roof, walk up walls, and remain unscathed by gun and sword. However, in the real world, our R&D team members had to win Vodafone's recognition through dedication and perseverance alone. This cooperation with Vodafone was a new starting point for us. Later, we succeeded in addressing other challenges and continued to win over customers with high standards.

Inviting Microwave Experts to Join Us

Thanks to what we had achieved to that point, we were able to stand on equal footing with established microwave product suppliers. However, we imported outdoor units (ODUs), which were a key component for our first generation of microwave products. As a result, we were less competitive in terms of power transmission, modulation, and performance. If we continued to rely on imported ODUs, we wouldn't be able to secure a position as a leader in the microwave industry.

Gao Ji, then-director of the Network Marketing Department, suggested that we go to Milan and look for microwave experts who could help us develop our own ODUs and gain a clear understanding of the future direction of the microwave industry. During our visit to Milan, we met Renato Lombardi, which turned out to be the most fruitful result of that trip.

One day not long before Christmas, we met Renato for the first time in a coffee shop, and we all felt good about the discussion. We talked about how to build the company's centre of expertise in the field of microwaves in Milan. Our conversation also covered how long it would take to build this centre of expertise, how much we should invest, and how many employees would have to be hired. After Renato joined our team, he began to tell other experts about Huawei and our microwave development platform. He also brought with him several microwave experts to join his team. These experts shared their experience relating to architecture design with us, and helped save us an enormous amount of time and effort.

The next thing we did was to hold a microwave technology seminar in Milan that lasted more than a week. The European experts had to attend the full sessions of the seminar and needed to work during the two-day holiday in Milan. Renato knew that he might get into trouble if he told his wife that he had to work and could not be with her during the holiday. So, he played a bit of a trick. Renato said to his wife, "I will travel to China on business and will most likely not be able to get back before Christmas." His wife was very upset. Two days later, however, Renato said to his wife, "I actually don't need to travel to China. My Chinese colleagues will be coming to Milan and we will have meetings here. The only thing is, I'll have to work over the two-day holiday." His wife was very happy to hear this and said, "It's great that you don't need to travel to China. It doesn't matter that you'll be working during the holiday. Just go ahead and do your work."

In 2009, when we were developing our own ODUs, Renato put forward a revolutionary design solution, which required laying out all the components on a single smaller PCB board rather than on two. Although this solution was much more competitive in terms of performance and cost, it was technically very hard and posed tougher challenges to the R&D team. With the help of the European experts, our R&D team in Xi'an discussed the new solution in depth for almost four hours. The conversation touched on the board layout, heat dissipation, size of each component, and sealing. Though there were some risks connected to the new solution, we still decided to adopt it.

Huawei's Stable ODUs

Developing ODUs was an even harder journey. As acknowledged by the industry, it was a challenge to design a super high-frequency circuit because of the challenges inherent in giving RF components the same frequency. ODUs were often used in harsh environments. For example, they had to be able to operate for long periods in areas subject to extreme temperatures, including deserts and areas covered by ice and snow, or in coastal areas with corrosive seawater. Quality was therefore of utmost importance.

The microwave technology seminar in Milan

Once, during one temperature cycle test, an ODU failed to start up. We became all the more anxious when the problem did not recur in the following days. One team member, who was responsible for locating the fault, could not take his eyes off the ODU, worrying that the fault would show itself the second he turned away. Then, one night, the ODU malfunctioned again when it was tested in a low temperature environment. The team member hurried to report this fault to the experts of the relevant departments so they could begin an analysis. Unfortunately, the ODU resumed normal operation again before we could locate the fault.

Over the following several days, the only option open to us was to try to get the fault to reoccur again. One night, it occurred when the testing temperature fell to -45°c. Employees from the departments of software, hardware, and RF were very excited and came to the climatic test chamber to analyse the fault based on what we had discussed earlier. We added more capacitors, changed the resistance and adjusted the component power-on time. Through this process, we were finally able to identify the root cause of the fault: there was something wrong with the component power-on time. We changed the time sequence, adjusted other related parameters and ultimately solved the problem.

Many companies could make a sample ODU unit. The bigger challenge was to mass-produce them. When we put the sample ODU into mass production, the first pass yield (FPY) was only 30%. We were shocked at the result and had to test, locate, and address each of the problems every day in a slow and tedious process. After about five months of significant effort, we increased the FPY to 85%. We still weren't satisfied with these results and continued to optimize the product. Finally, the FPY exceeded 95.4%, a number high enough to allow us to continue with mass production.

The final ODUs that we produced could operate stably without being affected by the climate, whether it be in the -45°c icy and snowy Arctic Circle, the steaming hot equator where temperatures rise to 50°c, the coastal areas with corrosive seawater in Latin America and India, or the high-altitude Himalayan region.

Microwave equipment in the desert

We had, thus, successfully developed our own ODUs, which enabled us to take the lead in terms of performance, power consumption, and quality, and we no longer needed to rely on other suppliers. In 2010, we produced an ODU sample unit and also launched the product to the market. We shattered the notion that Huawei could not produce its own sample ODU unit within two years.

Huawei's Self-Developed Chips

Every month, Huawei produced tens of thousands of sets of microwave equipment, which were sold worldwide to several billion users. However, the chips used in the equipment were not developed by Huawei.

Though it was a tough challenge to research and develop our own chips and algorithms, we decided to do it. We discussed this initiative with top suppliers of microwave chips. Their view was basically that "based on your current capabilities, you won't be able to make your own chips within a short period of time." These words were disappointing, but also energized us and made us more determined to have our own chips.

Renato joined forces with experts from our European Research Center, HiSilicon, and algorithm and product design teams to develop our own chips. We established a joint team made up of members from our Chengdu, Xi'an, and Milan offices.

We did not have the relevant technologies or experience to draw upon, which made the R&D process arduous. At the end of November 2010, with only one month left before the first self-developed modem chips were to be delivered, we found that the phase noise, phase jump, and other key indicators were lagging behind the specifications of the top suppliers of microwave chips. Therefore, it was unlikely that we could produce the chips and put them into commercial use as planned. We were obviously under great pressure.

During the last 21 days before the deadline, we analysed the performance of phase noise and phase jump, and finally put forward a solution based on the linear interpolation algorithm. Thanks to this solution, the chips performed much better than before and even surpassed the specifications of some top chip suppliers. By using an independently developed chip in our microwave equipment, we achieved major reductions in both cost and power consumption. In addition, we no longer had to rely exclusively on one single chip supplier.

Of course, just having a competitive product wasn't enough. If we didn't work on our delivery capabilities, then the more products we sold, the more problems we would run into. In 2011, we won a bid from Hutchison Indonesia involving the deployment of over 10,000 sets of microwave equipment. According to our agreement with the customer, we had three years to deliver this batch of product. However, the customer changed its mind and asked us to make a delivery within a year and a half. This was the first time we had handled such a big project. If there were only several hundred sets, we could manage the planning and changes through Excel. However, if we tried to manage a project with over 10,000 sets through Excel, the system could easily fail – even if we just performed an easy calculation.

Therefore, it was imperative for us to develop tools to manage project delivery. The team members involved in tool development were sent to sites and warehouses in Indonesia to identify the requirements relating to tools, and then wrote code for them. When we developed a function, we asked the project team on-site to test it and collected feedback. If the team members found the tool useful, we would arrange training for business partners on this tool and spread its use. We thus gradually developed a system of microwave tools and applied them to more than 100 projects worldwide, which greatly increased the efficiency of our project delivery for microwave products.

We successfully delivered the project to Hutchison Indonesia at the end of 2012. The company's CTO sent us a thankyou letter and, when I read it, tears began welling up in my eyes. We eventually achieved success, but it had been such a tough journey.

Huawei's microwave products enjoyed rapid development and success in the market thanks to the hard work of everyone involved. We have served almost every major operator worldwide and, by 2015, we had held the largest market share globally for three consecutive years. We realized our dream in just a few short years, much shorter than the normal microwave R&D process, which might sometimes require several decades. I feel so lucky to have been a part of our company's development of microwave products and to have witnessed how we developed from a newcomer, to a follower, and eventually to an industry leader. Life is short and I am grateful for having had such a valuable experience.

IP Eagles
in a
Data-Driven
World

By Gai Gang

'Chinese Chips' Set Youthful Hearts Ablaze

In 2000, I graduated from university at the age of 22. I then came to Shenzhen to join Huawei as a hardware engineer. I worked hard and I was soon promoted to project manager in charge of developing our S8500 series of switch products. That project achieved the goal of developing Huawei's first ever 10Gbit Ethernet interface for switches. In 2003, I was transferred to the Internet Protocol (IP) core router team, and I have now been working on IP routers for more than a decade.

When I started to work with IP, I realized that it is a very high-end technology. Even today, only a handful of manufacturers around the world have mastered this technology. Back in 2003, Huawei was racing to catch up with industry leaders. Our competitors were starting to market 40G routers, but Huawei was still selling old 10G and 20G products, because we just didn't have the technology. Customers weren't even considering us, and our sales colleagues out in local offices all over the world were very unhappy because the products were not competitive. We didn't have our own IP chipsets, so we had to buy them from Western suppliers. But the functions and specifications of the chipsets purchased were often a whole generation behind those of our competitors. So we were determined to develop our own 40G IP chipsets and master the core technologies ourselves.

The 40G chip was the crystallization of everything we knew about IP networking and our entire IP approach. To increase specifications and performance, we adopted new architectures, algorithms, multi-million-gate circuits, and the latest semiconductor manufacturing technologies in the industry. We also ran into unprecedented technological challenges.

Many new members joined our team, working in Beijing, Shenzhen, Chengdu, and overseas. We learned and developed as we worked. The whole team was battling to accelerate our algorithms for routing table entries and butting up against the limitations of physical design. We brought in experts and key employees from the chipset and software teams to tackle the knotty problems with us. For the first time, we combined chipset modelling and simulation with virtual layout and routing. We ran a full simulation and verification of the design solution, and finally managed to make the technological breakthrough we needed, which paved the way for us to develop and apply the actual chipsets.

By the end of 2009, the first batch of 40G chipset samples was ready for testing. We talked about how to approach it and decided to bring the whole batch to Shenzhen and upgrade our core routers with the new 'Chinese chips'. This would give a massive boost to our product competitiveness.

A week before the Chinese New Year, the first batch of 40G IP chipsets rolled off the production line and the team sent them quickly over to the Shenzhen R&D Lab for testing. We sat together in the lab, discussing and solving problems as they appeared. The lab was alternately a babble of voices and an area of deathly silence, save for the tapping of keyboards. At 11pm at night, the 40G IP chipset successfully forwarded its first data packet and after that we romped through the scenario tests one by one. Deep into the night, we were bubbling with excitement, running through all the tests we could. In the end, our boss came and chased us out of the lab. "You've passed all the key scenario tests," he said. "Go and get some sleep, and you can finish up tomorrow."

On the eve of Chinese New Year, Zha Jun, president of the company's Fixed Network Product Line, ushered in the New Year with us at a hotel near the company. He brought his parents, wife and daughter along to the dinner, and he and his little four-year-old girl treated us to a rousing duet of the Chinese national anthem. We all sang along, louder and louder as we went, and a number of us became quite emotional. It was a night of laughter and tears, with plenty of drink and singing. A traditional time for family, a group of passionate young people, and a vision of strong Chinese chipset powering core routers ... something sparked that cold winter night and set our youthful hearts ablaze.

On New Year's Day, we went out to the Overseas Chinese Town, one of Shenzhen's more laid-back locations. But the break was soon over, and the next day we threw ourselves back into the battle of chipset testing. On the eighth day of the Chinese New Year, the first working day after the holiday, we delivered Huawei's first generation of IP chipsets for core network routers, right on schedule.

The performance of our Chinese chipset was comparable to those of global industry leaders and significantly improved the competitiveness of our router hardware. We had made many breakthroughs and mastered the underlying technologies. We were poised to make an attempt at the very top spot in the chip industry and paved the way for future development of chipsets up to 400G and beyond.

It has been a good few years now, but I still remember that holiday we spent together, the songs we sang, the New Year dinner we shared, and the days that we struggled through, side by side.

2010 Chinese New Year Dinner

Joining the Exclusive 'Cluster Club'

We moved on, and new challenges rolled in. Huawei was building the core nodes of China Telecom's national backbone network, and we thus needed new technology. I was responsible for this product category, so I was given a new mission: delivering a cluster router within a single year.

A core node in the national backbone network is the regional information hub. Data streams from multiple provinces and cities converge there and radiate out, so the torrents of data are enormous. Even more challenging is the fact that the data flow is still growing by 50% every year. A single chassis (server cabinet) could not handle the increasing volumes of information that flow through a core node, so we would have to connect multiple chassis in a cascading manner to form a large cluster that could support the growth and evolution of the network. For a long time, US companies had dominated the market for multiple-chassis cluster systems, and American products were used in the national backbone networks of many countries. The multiple-chassis cluster is the most complicated IP system, and router clusters represent the pinnacle of technology for any equipment manufacturer. Cluster technology is the Mount Everest of IP tech.

This was a key project for the company, and we were given all the support we needed. To develop the router architecture, we quickly called in a dozen experts in a range of fields: Zang Dajun, the hardware expert; Keely Yang, the switching network expert; Zhou Da, the processing expert; Edmond Van and Mao Xuefeng, software service engineers; and Dustin Tian, the Mechanical Power Environment (MPE) expert. We gathered in a meeting room in the Beijing Research Center, with seven or eight computers and a couple of whiteboards, and we got to sketch out the architecture for router clusters.

Router clusters are a huge technical challenge. You have to take what was originally a group of independent devices and integrate them into an '8+64' cluster. The complexity of both the hardware and software increases by several orders of magnitude.

Our existing knowledge and architecture would not produce the results we needed, so we had to start from scratch. We had little or no guidance, so all we could do was hope that the impressive experience that our expert team brought to the table would spark something. Whiteboard space became our most scarce resource. Over and again, someone would have an idea, draw it up and, if it didn't work, wipe it off. For a month, we bounced ideas off each other, and finally we developed a proposal that we could show to an IP expert, the Huawei Fellow, Deng Chaojun. Deng reviewed our idea and approved it, and at that moment Huawei's own router cluster architecture came into being.

However, product development proved to be much harder than we had imagined. We had to invent many technologies: the cluster central chassis, cascaded optical fibres, trunk control plane, and distributed computing. Each one of these was new to us and presented many problems to be overcome. When the first batch of central chassis was produced, design errors caused bent pins in many of the boards, and quite a few boards did not work at all. We had to stop and wait for the problem to be resolved. The underlying VxWorks operating system did not support cluster operations, so we had to switch and adapt a lot of the software. As the number of system boards in the cluster increased, software performance kept dropping off, so we had to optimize the software over and over again.

We kept supporting and encouraging each other through the hard times, reminding ourselves that: "There are only four countries in the world that can launch satellites; there are currently only two US companies in the world that can make router clusters of this complexity. If we can make our own router cluster, we will become one of the three members of the 'cluster club'. That's pretty impressive!" Every time we ran into difficulties or felt like giving up, we thought of being part of that exclusive club and powered on through.

You might call it delusional; you might call it boastful; you might think it was a pipe dream. But whatever it was, it was a goal, and goals are what we fight for. When a boast turns into reality, we see that it was actually visionary; but boasting alone won't get you there. It takes blood, sweat, and tears, every step of the way.

An integrated test on a cluster of routers demands hundreds or thousands of ports and a large number of meters and instruments. We had limited resources, so the project team split into two shifts to keep the equipment running 24/7. Even at night, our passion for work remained undimmed. At first, we only had instant noodles to keep us going through the small hours. Then the parents of Tao Chun, who was managing the hardware tests, came to Shenzhen to visit him. They were from the cold northeast of China, famous for its hearty, filling food. They would make a pan of New Year wraps and bring them to the Huawei front gate at 9.30pm every night. Tao would pick them up and bring them to the lab for us all to share. Every day, regular as clockwork, our nightly meal would arrive. Everyone loved the wraps, and there became a saying in our team: "Eat a plateful of wraps, solve a plateful of problems." After we finally completed the project, we missed those wraps most of all.

During that critical period, my daughter was born. In the hospital, I was of course thrilled to see my first child, but couldn't help worrying about the project schedule. I was glued to the phone even in the hospital, and my wife told me, "Get back to the company to check on your 'child'. My parents can take care of me and the baby. You concentrate on your work!" With the support of my wife, I went back to work immediately. My colleagues were surprised to see me, asking, "What are you doing back so soon?" I answered matter-of-factly: "I have another 'child' to look after here. I can't leave this 'child' alone." Actually, everyone saw this product as our baby. We were completely devoted to this project. And it was only possible because of the understanding and support from our families.

The development of the cluster was much more difficult than we had imagined. The project schedule had to be repeatedly pushed back, until the sales department finally sent out an internal memo requesting that we hurry up because we had to meet the deadline for that year's procurement tests, which were to be carried out by the major telecom carriers. The pressure was officially on. Procurement tests are like China's national college entrance examination: the date is fixed, and you only get one chance. Only products that pass the test will be bought by the carriers and used in their networks for the next year. If you don't make it, then you have to sit on the sidelines until next year's tests.

If we failed the test, we would miss the opportunity to supply China Telecom's backbone network project. That would be an enormous blow for the whole team. But, as the saying goes, 'he who dares, wins'. We rose to the challenge that the sales team set us and unveiled our router cluster on time at the Guangdong Institute of Telecommunications. The next three months were a high-stress period of testing, but we were able to handle everything that was thrown at us, and finally we received the credentials we needed to become a part of the national backbone network. We were now officially a member of the exclusive club of just three companies in the world with the capacity to build router clusters.

To this day, my wife still makes fun of me, and asks, "How is your 'child' doing at work?" I tell her that my 'child' is performing brilliantly. We staked our first claim on the core nodes of China's backbone network when China Telecom Xi'an successfully installed the world's first '2+4' core router cluster. In 2013, we pulled off the world's biggest cluster upgrade, when China Unicom hired us to replace the China '1.69' backbone node in Wuxi. This project showed that, in addition to building our own new systems, Huawei had the ability to swap out and replace existing clusters.

Today, our router clusters are everywhere, in the core nodes of operators and in the national backbone networks. We have become an indispensible part of the China backbone network. But I would like to say thank you to my family, and to the families of every member of the project team. Without your understanding and support, we could not have made it through the hard times. We could never have created one of the world's most advanced pieces of IP cluster technology. Half of our success is yours.

There are some
achievements that
stick in the mind.
There are some
people who
command
your respect.

An Operating System Thoroughly Refined

There are some achievements that stick in the mind. There are some people who command your respect.

To make a powerful IP network, one of the other key elements you need is the versatile routing platform (VRP) operating system that runs on routers. Upgrading hardware is all very well, but software must keep pace.

The next-generation operating system was to be VRP8, but during the initial development phase, we got stuck in round after round of discussions. Some of the software specialists thought that we should evolve the system we had. Others thought that the old system would never be able to support the new performance demands of customer networks, and that we needed to start afresh. We examined the merits of each viewpoint very carefully and made a considered decision: we should develop a new system. The new system would become the basis for long-term development of our IP systems and would be a next-generation software platform for our network equipment.

Twenty-one system architecture engineers gathered at the Beijing Research Center and began to design the architecture. Every engineer wrote a commitment to the project, and they were all displayed in nice crystal frames. Each one of them said, "I hereby promise to commit myself 100% to developing the very highest quality system architecture for VRP8 and to take lifelong responsibility for it."

The team came from many different parts of the country, and each of us was a recognized expert in our own field. These software champions had a natural competitive energy, and they turned that system architecture into a work of art. Over and again, they sculpted and streamlined it, each one of them pursuing quality to the point of perfection. The review process that they set up brought a whole new meaning to the word 'excellence', as they ruthlessly eliminated even the tiniest of flaws. Every time they reviewed each other's latest progress, they would push the bar a little higher. Every decision would be questioned again and again, until the presenter didn't have any answers left. Some of the team members weren't used to this rough treatment and would storm out of the meeting room to refine and perfect their work so that next time they could deflect every possible attack.

In the summer of 2010, the VRP8 system faced its first major test: a limited pilot deployment in Jinan, the capital city of Shandong Province. The sales teams were watching this first deployment of VRP8 with great interest. We thought it best to calm any worries the customer might have about being the first to try out this new product, so several members of our R&D team went to Jinan to explain the product to the customer. We talked to the customer about how advanced and reliable the new VRP8 was, and about our plans for mitigating any risks. In the end, the customer agreed to the installation. In the early hours of 9 September 2010, we switched over the China Telecom Jinan network to the world's first VRP8 system, and it smoothly took up the load. This successful start proved that the VRP8 system was up to the challenge of real-world operations and was a great boost to the confidence of our team.

At the end of 2010, we loaded VRP8 onto our core routers and presented it for the first time to major Chinese operators at their annual group procurement tests. In the areas of testing where we had always underperformed in the past, such as convergence time and switchover time, we outshone every other product there. From its very conception, we always meant for VRP8 to become a top performer among all of the world's IP network operating systems. And our high standards and stringent quality demands meant that we hit every one of the targets that we shot for. Many of the architects who were part of that team still get excited just at the thought of what we achieved together.

Focus, Persevere, Breakthrough: The Road to 400 Gigabit

At the end of 2011, I became the president of Huawei's router product line. The biggest issue in front of me was how to make the next breakthrough.

We had to handle enough data to feed high-definition televisions (4K and 2K) and flows of data to and from the cloud. Operators were demanding increasingly high bandwidth, and we had to supply them with data pipes big enough to carry whole oceans of data. Since we had been investing heavily in chipsets, software operating systems, and router clusters for over a decade, we were ready to become a world leader in R&D. The only question was, could we live up to the challenge? Could we turn those years of investment into new breakthroughs, and realize the ambitions of generations of our IP engineers for surpassing the industry benchmark?

In the summer of 2012, Beijing was in the grip of a heatwave. Near the Beijing Research Center, at the foot of some large hills, lies the Temple of Great Awakening. It has stood there for centuries, red walls and green trees, an oasis of calm. This was where we met to discuss our plans to surpass the industry benchmark. We brought together the management of the sales teams, marketing, and R&D, for a session of vigorous debate.

The marketing team had analysed our competition and believed that if we could bring a 400G router to market six months earlier than we had originally planned, we could take a commanding position in the core router market. To many, this sounded impossible. There was just too much to do. We could never shave six months off the delivery time.

At the end of a day of vigorous discussion, the product team agreed that ten years of efforts on IP chipsets and software operating systems had given us the R&D capacity to take a world-leading position. Even if the marketing team projected that we were only 50% confident in getting ahead of others, we still committed ourselves to making this push. After all, if we missed this opportunity, we would regret it forever.

We decided to drop everything unrelated to the 400G router project, and focus all our R&D resources on it. We would make it to market six months ahead of schedule, or even earlier, and we would take the market position Huawei wanted in 400G.

At the end of the meeting, we shared a vegetarian meal at the temple. It tasted better than steak to us, because we had made a commitment and we thus glimpsed the possibility of success. Just before we left, we posed for a group photograph at the temple gates. If we succeeded in this 400G mission, we vowed to remember that this was the moment that we started.

At the current rate of progress, the 400G router was not due to be ready for delivery until the second half of 2013. Now we had shifted the delivery date to May. Undoubtedly, this was a mammoth task that we had given to the R&D team. It meant that we only had one shot at every phase. The 400G chipset had to be right the first time; the boards had to be right the first time; and our software development process had to be massively accelerated. In order to meet the new schedule, our R&D team set the target of having 'zero adjustment, zero wait time, and zero errors'.

We wrote ourselves a slogan, "One team, one dream," to draw together the chipset side and the board team, and remind ourselves that we were part of the same effort. Paul Nadj, a Canadian system architect, liked to say, "When we run into a problem, we have to take a step back and think about what the heart of the problem is and what the cause is. We carry out an analysis to find the major pain point, then we blast it." Painstaking work led us quickly to solutions to the key technical issues and meant that quality was built in from the beginning. That laid the foundation for turning the chipset technology into products.

On 8 October 2012, the 400G chipset arrived at our Shenzhen lab. After nine hours of booting and testing, our chipset was ready, and everyone was very excited. On 25 October, in the same lab, we called together the driver software, chip, forwarding software, and higher-level software teams, and the commissioning began. The minutes and hours flew by. On day one, the CPU mini system booted up, and on day two we got the network processor functional. But when we came to the traffic management module, we got stuck. The whole team of experts crowded around the whiteboard, running through the protocols line by line, analysing and checking each one, to eliminate every possible problem. Finally, every issue was resolved, and the module integrated smoothly into the system. We watched the meters jump as they recorded packets sent and received, and as the "lost packet" counter settled and sat firmly at 0, our fists shot into the air and we whooped in excitement.

In May 2013, seven months ahead of schedule, our 400G router was officially launched to the markets, a full year and a half in advance of our competitors.

In August of that same year, the first 400G router went into service in Saudi Arabia, sending shockwaves through the operator world. An expert assessment concluded that a single Huawei NE5000E Cluster Router unit offered the same capacity as a 2+4 cluster of 100G routers, while using just one-eigth of the energy, occupying one-sixth of the space, and weighing just one-twelfth as much. In terms of availability, we had 18 months on anyone else in the industry. This was Huawei's best-ever result, and it put us at the forefront of the technology race.

The 400G router was a reliable, high-quality piece of equipment, with superior line capacity, high performance, and low power consumption. It quickly became the most common piece of equipment on China's high-end data lines, ending China's reliance on Western suppliers for core routers and stunning the global communications market.

The Huawei 400G router is now used in over 60 nations and regions on five continents. It now serves over a billion people. The success of the 400G router was made possible because we were bold enough to seize the opportunity. It came about because we made sustained investment, and at crunch time we persevered until the victory was ours. For more than a decade, several generations of IP engineers committed their time and effort to key technologies, and our financial investment was heavy. Ultimately, when opportunity came knocking, we were able to surpass the competition and lead the market.

"The telecom industry is a cruel master. You never know what is coming tomorrow, or next month."

Youth, Passion, Ambition

At the Mobile World Congress 2016, Huawei presented its latest generation of routers, the petabit-rated NE9000, and the world's first 2 Terabit router line card. I saw the CEOs and CTOs of the biggest telecom operators in the world stop in front of our product display, listen to the Huawei experts explaining product functionality and then express their admiration and appreciation. I couldn't help but feel proud. The breakthroughs we have made in chipsets and many other key technologies have made Huawei a trailblazer in IP networking technology.

Looking back over my career, I see now that it was just blind chance that I ended up working in IP technology. I certainly never expected to be working in this same field for more than a decade. Over these years, we have kept up a high level of investment of both time and energy in IP chipsets, software operating systems, cluster technology, and other key technical features. We have fought to catch up with our competitors. We have doubled down when the going got tough. We have focused and persevered and, when the opportunity came, we made our breakthrough. We became the leader in 400G. Today, I feel a combination of pride and satisfaction, but also a measure of resignation.

I have heard people say that, "The telecom industry is a cruel master. You never know what is coming tomorrow, or next month." I didn't believe it at the time. Now that I have been through it myself, I finally understand what they meant. This is an industry that combines the highest levels of technology, fierce competition and a startling pace of change. Every player swaggers in with a bellyful of confidence and some exciting weapons in their arsenal. But how many of them last? I have been thinking hard about what factors contributed to our success. What was it that inspired us to stay so dedicated, when the rewards were so uncertain? What keeps us just as committed, over ten years later, as the day we first started?

I believe that Huawei has created a great stage upon which we can develop. Huawei has accepted the costs that growth inevitably incurs. The company makes the investment, delivers the resources and gives us the space to play out Huawei's IP fairytale. I believe that the love in our hearts, the families who support us, and the colleagues who inspire us create a haven of warmth and mutual encouragement, enabling us to cope with isolation, overcome hurdles, and embrace our bold vision.

I believe that when a group of ambitious young people come together, committed to devoting their youth and energy to making a new and world-class product, then they will never shrug away from any hardship, exhaustion, or problems, and they will not stop at anything to attain their goals.

We are young. We are the eagles on the crags who choose the sky, always that farther patch of bluer-than-blue sky ...

The Huawei router exhibition booth at the Mobile World Congress 2016

Editors

Biography
of Tian Tao

Tian Tao is a member of the Huawei International Advisory Council, Co-Director of the Ruihua Institute for Innovation Management at Zhejiang University in Hangzhou, China and a Visiting Fellow at Cambridge Judge Business School.

In 1991, Tian Tao founded *Top Capital*, the first Chinese magazine on private equity investment, and has served as Editor in Chief since.